The Secret Of A Much Longer Life: And More Pleasure In Living It

Goddard Ezekiel Dodge Diamond

The Secret of a Much Longer Life

AND MORE PLEASURE IN LIVING IT

Born in Plymouth, Mass., May 1, 1796

Living on Eighth Street, San Francisco, Cal.,
May 1, 1906

DEDICATION

After more than one hundred and ten years of active life, in possession and perfect use of every sense, and faculty unimpaired,

I DEDICATE THIS BOOK

To the cause of temperance in all things, knowing that proper care of the body, and selection and use of nature's food and drink, are the only means of arriving at old age, healthy and happy.

Better Luck to San Francisco, California.

In sadness do I now look back
Upon the bygone days,
When I was happy all day long
In boyish sports and ways;
But now I'm forced to make my way,
One hundred and ten years, as you see,
Those prosperous and good old times
Will come no more to me.
I little thought, as time flew by,
Misfortune thick and fast
Would o'er me fall and make me to
Suffer misfortune to the last.
Such is my lot! Wealth can't replace
For loss of (my government papers) to me,
A government agent no more I'll be.
And now my thoughts once more return
To boyhood's happy days,
And to the familiar haunts,
I often wish I might return
To my old home once more.
But friends are gone—I try to live
To meet them on yon shore.
And now, dear friends, I'm as you see,
Poor, helpless and alone,
No other way to earn my bread,
Will you please buy my book!
The Secret of a Longer Life and
More pleasure in living it.

CAPT. G. E. DIAMOND, Author of the Book.

Sent to your address postpaid for (50) cents by the author, one hundred and ten years old the 1st of May. 1906.

Residence, 716 20th street, Oakland, California.

GODDARD E. D. DIAMOND (AT AGE 110)

A SPECIAL WRITER DOUBTS.

"There is an old man living in this city, his name is Diamond, his age is given by himself as 103 years. As respect is naturally due to one whitened by the passing of many seasons, the feeling toward the venerable Diamond could hardly fall short of reverence. There is something august about the man who has braved the storms of a century, who stands at last alone at the head of a path marked on either side by the graves of generations, born, matured and in fullness of time gathered to their fathers while the solitary figure has survived, a living link between the present and a past that is dead. Yet, in the case of Diamond, I would like to see the proofs. He looks to be a well-preserved man of 80. Supposing that inadvertently he has added a score of years to his record, the mistake would be hard to detect. He has never married, and therefore there are no relatives who might serve as a check. Living so solitary a life as he has, even if no more than 80, there would be great difficulty in controverting any statement he might make in relation to this matter. I do not wish to cast any reflection upon the old man. He may be sincere, but there are the delusions of age to be considered. He may even be correct. But in a stage of the world at which the man of 80 is rare, the man of 90 a wonder the centenarian little less than a miracle, my stock of faith is overtaxed by the effort to accept this hale and vigorous Diamond, exhibiting the promise of living for decades to come, as having been ushered into this world in 1796. If he was, he can reasonably expect to be here in 1996, a marvel to races yet to be."

AN ARTISTS OPINION.

"During April 1896, my friend told me that I ought to get a sitting of a gentleman who would complete a century of life on the coming first of May. The rarity of persons attaining the age of one hundred years excited my interest, and I agreed to make a life-size direct portrait of the centenarian if my friend would bring him to my studio on his one hundredth birthday anniversary.

"Naturally, expecting so old a gentleman to be very feeble, on the day appointed for the sitting, I made preparations accordinglv. I covered my skylight with cloth, thinking that eyes at that age would not be able to stand the light. I remember, also, placing an easy chair ready for the sitting. Presently my friend came in, with another gentleman, and announced the arrival of Mr. Diamond. I asked them to have the old gentleman's carriage driven round into the court, when, to my great astonishment, my friend introduced the gentleman with him as Captain Diamond, himself. I was dumbfounded! Here was a man standing straight as a young prince, moving with an elastic, sprightly step, and with a bright, youthful twinkle shining in his eye! I could see, at once, that I had gone to too much unnecessary trouble in my preparations. Photographers are often obliged to refuse direct sittings for large portraits, and instead enlarge from small pictures, because of the inability of the subject to remain perfectly quiet for the requisite length of time. In spite of his great age, there was not the slightest difficulty of this kind with Mr. Diamond. He certainly is the best sitter I ever had. During the long exposure necessary to insure the quality in a direct life-size portrait, he never moved a particle. Every hair of his head and of beard came out as sharp as in any other sitting I ever made of a man of thirty, no matter how much I braced the latter up with back and head rest. Even today, I will agree to make life-size direct sittings of Mr. Diamond at twenty-five cents each above cost, and for every one I miss on account of his moving I will forfeit ten dollars. Come forward, ye who doubt!

"I was asked to copy a tintype of Mr. Diamond, taken in the year 1861, at the age of sixty-five years. It looks much older than he does today. The shoulders are unevenly sloped and bent forward, the eyes sunken, the thin, fine hair all gone, while the thick, vigorous hair forms a distinct line about the face. These marks of age are missing now. He is erect, square-shouldered, and has a military bearing.

JOHN R. HODSON."

SAN FRANCISCO, Cal., March 16, 1896.

CLINICAL EXAMINATION.

PULSE TRACING.

Goddard Ezekiel Dodge, Diamond, born in Plymouth, Mass., May 1, 1796. Lived nearly all his life in the United States. Made several trips to the West Indias, living there a few months at a time. Has visited the European continent; never resided in the tropics. Has had very little illness in his life. Yellow fever once; pneumonia once. Has been asphyxiated twice from charcoal fumes. Met with numerous accidents; bones broken, left shoulder dislocated. Height, 5 feet 6 1-4 inches. Present weight, 141 pounds. Nine years ago he weighed 225 pounds Reduced himself by diet. Appetite always good; digestion excellent. Diet plain; no sweets, no meats, since 1852. Never used a stimulant of any kind; never used tobacco. Drink hot water thrice daily; no tea, no coffee. Temperment passive. Uses olive oil external and internal. Never been married. Keeps the same weight. No difficulty in breathing. Can lie in any position, preferring an abdominal one. No palpitation. Visceral functions normal. Virility good. Pulse regular in rhythm, tension slight, easily compressible, irregularly intermittent; walls of vessel at the wrist slightly atheromatous; temporal artery same as radical except atheroma. Pulse rate 76. Respiration regular, full 18. Vision good; reaction of pupils normal; range of vision somewhat shortened, reading a ten-foot chart short at 8 feet. Physical appearance good, resembling a well-preserved man of 78. Absence of wrinkles; face slightly flushed; condition of the skin in all parts of the body excellent, except over the abdomen, which shows the loss of tissue, owing to the great reduction in weight. Hair gray, not bald. Chest well formed with exception of a deep depression in the lower sternal region, which has persisted since youth. Marked prominence of the ensiform cartilage, which is almost bifid at its extremity. Marked prominence of the sternal angles of the ribs, probably due to contraction from ossification of the costal cartilages. Chest 36 inches around breast line, expansion very limited, 1 3-4 of an inch. This seems due more to the rigidity of the chest walls than from any lack of expansion of the lung tissue Abdominal 34 inches. Expansion 1 inch. Thigh firm, 16½ inches. Arm 9½ inches. Wrist 6¼ inches. Legs are firm, slight in build; calf 13 inches; absence of all varicosity. **Blood**—Density of corpuscle slightly increased; haemaglobin reduced; morphology of red cells almost normal; some fields numerous mishappen cells. **Kidney reaction**—Very fair; amount of urine passed in 24 hours, 46 to 50 ounces. Acid, cloudy; urea in excess; sp. gravity, 1026; chlorine, high; albumen, none; large excess of bile; urates, abundant; tube casts, absent; some bladder epithelium.

The physical examination of Capt. Diamond reveals a remarkable preservation of tissue integrity and function activity. There is no factor or combination of factors which would suggest any approach to dissolution; and if the same vegetable routine of life is maintained, and no intercurrent complication supervenes, it would be purely speculative to hazard an opinion as to the probable future span of life.

The dangers more directly suggested by his proposed walk from San Francisco to New York would be too much mental strain from excitement and anxiety for the success of his undertaking, and probable stress upon the circulatory system when mountain climbing.

FREDERICK Wm. D'EVELYN.

SAN FRANCISCO, March 22, 1898.

(Dr. D'Evelyn is a graduate of Edinburg University and head physician of St. Luke's Hospital, San Francisco.)

WHY I PUBLISH THIS BOOK.

The attention of the reader is called to the article on the preceding pages from the pen of a special writer for a daily paper (editorial page). The article may have been inspired by an interview in the office of that paper's artist the week previously, when, by request, I permitted a sketch to be made of myself.

My friends tell me that the special writer for that paper voices the opinion of all strangers whom I meet. In justice to my claims, for which I have given my word, and as an example to this fast age in which we are living, it seems to me a duty to furnish evidence of my claims, and an example of the value of temperance in all things.

If the reader would understand the gist of this little book clearly, it is well for him to study with some care the introduction by the well-known artist of San Francisco, Prof. J. R. Hodson, in his reference to the three pictures of the subject of this sketch. He very clearly points out the lines of contrast which mark the signs of "old age," and in the comparison shows, from an artist's standpoint, that the age of decline had set in, that it was arrested, and more than thirty-five years later the subject exhibited a younger form and more healthy appearance than at the age of 65. Attention is especially called to the clinical examination by a well-known physician.

This may seem to the casual reader but idle

speculation, but to the facts I bear witness, and that from personal experience. It is as plain to me as is the road to the traveler over which he has come slowly. Nor is it simply a case of inheritance and as a matter of course—but rather is it the result of a life of denial to the palate, and of good care to the framework of this body.

BIOGRAPHICAL.

If I live until the first day of May, 1900, I will celebrate my one hundred and fourth birthday anniversary, since I first saw the light in Plymouth, Massachusetts.

Four years ago I crossed the threshold of the second century of my experience in the flesh, and am now in the enjoyment of as good health as when in my thirties or forties.

There is not a pain disturbing my body; not a joint ailing from rheumatic twinges; not a languid feeling of the nervous system; not a sign of heavy hearing. At 48 I was a very feeble old man. In 1852 I had yellow fever in Apalachicola, Florida. My experience justifies the opinion that it is possible for man to live into the second century of this life, and enjoy it all the way through with the bound of rising youth—retaining every faculty and enjoying every experience.

The personal request of my friends, as well as the many letters which have come to me recently from those who know me, as well as from many who know of me, asking me to write a book detailing the way and means by which I have attained such unusual longevity, lead me to write, in brief, my life experience, giving some reminiscences of myself, some men I have known and some events through which I have passed—summing it all up by telling the inquiring world how I got there over the corduroy roads without jarring the carriage into pieces.

Most people desire to know how to grow old gracefully, but my limited experience has taught me that it is a more desirable thing to grow old in the enjoyment of every faculty unimpaired, keeping in harmony with the changing condition of things, instead of quarreling with the innovations of up-to-date times because they are not as they used to be—or, what is better, not to grow old at all.

The road over which I have come was not made smooth by a pioneer corps, but it has been my privilege to help open the ways and lay the planks over which to pass to solid ground.

Some have questioned the certainty of my many years, for the reason that they do not bear down upon me as upon the great majority of our race. To meet that doubt it has occurred to me that I should record the years and events through which I have passed, as we used to blaze our way through the woods.

True, the inquirer will find it difficult to verify the facts set forth, by living men, yet the names of all I shall mention may be found on the records of city, county, state or military reports of their day, or on the slabs of marble where they have long since taken up their abode in the silent city of the dead. I will try to tell the reader in simple words the way I came and how I got there.

MY EARLIEST RECOLLECTIONS.

My father's family record showed tha I was born in Plymouth, Massachusetts, the first day of May, Seventeen hundred and ninety-six. My parents were Joseph and Mahala Diamond.

The Diamonds were of Scottish ancestry, and my father was of the first American generation, who lived to a ripe old age and died at Huntsville, Alabama, in eighteen hundred and Sixty-five.

My mother's maiden name was Allen, and she was a niece of General Ethan Allen of Ticonderoga fame. Her ancestry on her mother's side were the Cottons, who came over in the Mayflower. So it appears that in my veins run the blood of the Scotch, Irish, Dutch and English, about as desirable mixture as one can wish for ancestry.

In the first year of my life my father removed from Plymouth to the Province of Massachusetts, now known as Oxford County, State of Maine. In that heavily timbered country I grew up to young manhood, unseen and not seeing; assisting my father to fell the trees, pile up and burn brush, clear off the land and till the earth for a living, until he returned from the war of 1812, which I believe was in the year 1814, at which time he gave me my freedom and sent me out empty-handed. These early days of my life were so concealed from the public, and the world so unknown to me, that scarcely an event ocurred outside of the routine of farm life to impress my mind until the war of 1812 with the English, which made the first indellible impression upon my understanding. To be sure, I can call to mind our log-cabin among the timbers, our crude utensils and implements for farming, and our methods of tilling the earth.

When I was about ten years old I was lying on a bridge spanning a brook running through our farm, looking at the little fish sporting in the water beneath me. It was in early spring, when the snow was yet on the hillside and the ice was breaking up in the streams. While looking at the fish I was musing upon their hard life, living in cold water, and so I resolved not to catch any more fish lest I add to their hardships. Suddenly there came a stroke upon my back, like the slap of the open palm of a boy's hand. I sprang up, and believing that the boy had run to the hill-side, rushed up there to wash his face in the snow. No signs of a boy's tracks nor of a boy in person nor by proxy were visible. While looking around, a crash like the breaking of timbers came from the direction of the bridge, and looking back, I discovered that the ice gorge had broken loose and carried with it every timber of the bridge on which I had been reclining. The stroke on my back, like the hand of a boy, was a great mystery to me and gave me no little thought about the source from whence it came, but for which I have always been thankful, otherwise I should not have lived to tell the story, but of one thing I am sure, and that is that no material hand slapped me upon the back, or I should have found the owner before he could get out of sight.

After my father returned from the war of 1812, I came out of the wilderness and stopped twelve months at Yarmouth, Province of Massachusetts, after which I went to Boston, when, to my understanding, daylight dawned and time became to me as of the essence of life.

Before that I knew nothing, and of nothing except the routine of pioneer farm life. Nor do I despise the lowly life through which I passed my early years on the farm. It is quite probable that I owe much of my life-long health to the simple, industrious habits, swinging the ax, digging with the hoe, mixing with the earth and breathing the pure air.

My loss of early education met with some compensation in escaping the poisonous air of our modern day school-rooms, and the retaining of my nervous system intact, instead of being wrecked with an excited pressure of education stuffing to meet the demands of the text-book, to the exclusion of the application of common sense. Blessed is the youth who enjoys the privilege of country life, runs barefoot, and wades every creek and pond in the community.

It is quite unnecessary to tell the reader that my early education was sadly neglected. While on the farm with father, no such things talking of or trying to get an education came into our lives. Neither books nor periodicals of any kind were received in our home nor circulated in the community.

When I left the country, and went to Boston after the war, at about nineteen years of age, I did not know a letter of the alphabet. I recall my feeling of shame and mortification lest some one should discover my entire ignorance of letters. Every circular or printed matter of any kind upon which I could lay my hands, and honestly appropriate, was seized upon, kept in privacy, and as opportunity afforded studied over and absorbed in my understanding.

Steady application at last gave me a fair ability to read, and my penmanship became legible, so much so that during the four years of my service as "Chief Government Agent" in the Quartermaster and Commissary Department at St. Louis, I kept my own books, and was able in an hour's time to render a report of any transportation of men or supplies. I recall the consuming desire to know as much as possible from the world of letters. Every opportunity was seized upon to gather information with the eagerness of the busy bee in quest of the sweets possessed by the hundreds of flowers to which it has access. The most favorable opportunity which I had was my trips twice a year on a sailing vessel, the one in the spring on my migration from north to south, and the other upon my return in the spring again to the north. This line of thought and practice can be understood only by those who lived in early days, long before every city and hamlet had its free library, and before newspapers could be had upon the streets and at its corners. To the average man there were no books, no periodicals, no daily papers, no exchange of views by correspondence with learned men, and no such thing as an association with men who had the advantage of a liberal education. I kept my eyes and ears open, and used my pen all I could and devoured anything I could get my eyes upon or into my hands.

MY LIFE PRIOR TO THE CIVIL WAR.

Already much has been related of my early, boyish life in my first recollections, assisting in clearing off our land and scratching for a living.

From the paternal roof I went to a small community called Yarmouth, where I lighted like an unfledged birdling, stopping lost in its first flight. Here I spent twelve months to catch a breath and to gather sufficient courage to go to Boston.

Then and there began a migratory life, half north and half south, spending my summers in Massachusetts and New York and my winters in Florida and Mississippi, generally at New Orleans, with the exception of an occasional trip to the West Indies and the continent of Europe. My employment for many successive years was such as came to the lot of all men who were not provided with either a trade or an education in early life.

In this alternating way of living I spent the time from 1814, until 1852, when I was in Florida, at Apilachicola, where I was taken with the yellow fever. I was conveyed to New Orleans in the old steamer "America," thence to Cincinnati in the steamer "Hiram Powers," where I stopped at the Burnett House.

While in the South I was employed in commission business or superintending plantations. And when in the North, I was engaged in building the first railroads in the United States, among them being the railroad from Worcester to Boston, the Old Colony Road from Boston to Plymouth, the road from Albany to old Durripp, now Schenectady. Also my work was in the constructing of canals, levees and so forth. I took part in the construction of the Albany and Erie Canal, from Albany to Buffalo, which I twice assisted to enlarge. The Columbia Bottom Levee in Missouri, Madison County Levee of Illinois and Missouri, the Pacific Railroad, S. W. Branch and North Missouri, and the Iron Mountain Railroad were among those I engaged in constructing.

When the war began, in April of 1861, I was in St. Louis, engaged in the building of the Lexington and Farmer City Railroad. As I look back over that long period of long ago (aggregating sixty-five years of my life) and then look at men alongside of me who say that they are now sixty-five years old, it seems an incredible thing that my age then was more than three score years.

LOSS OF PAPERS.

Having lived a life of celibacy and all ancestry kindred long since gone, the links in my chain of life depend for solder upon direct papers as evidence of historic events which associate me with the history of others or with incidents or accidents in life. Very valuable papers bearing upon my life to my fortieth and fiftieth years, and all of the kind which I had, were lost, together with all of my effects, in the wrecking of two ships. The first was in the early forties of this century, when I was passenger on the brig "Mohegan," Captain Bell commanding, running from New Orleans to New York City. The ship foundered on the Ocracoke breakers, at the mouth of the Roanoke River, a dense fog prevailing. No lives were lost and no baggage was saved. Every-thing in the way of private papers, including a book, biographical, of the General Ethan Allen family, a branch of my ancestry (and which I have not been able to duplicate) went down in the wreck and never was recovered.

The second wreck to which I have referred, was that of "The Swallow," a steamer plying between Albany and New York City, on the North River. I was anxious to leave for New York that night. Two steamers were going, "The Diamond" and "The Swallow." I preferred the former, but could not get it. I was hastening to board "The Swallow" when some invisible but restraining hand checked me, until my impatience assumed anger, and, as if tearing away from restraint I stepped upon the plank and was drawn on board with it. After getting on board, a second sober thought caused me to review the strange incident on land, and it so impressed me that I resolved not to go to my berth until the steamer had passed the "Highlands" and was well out upon broader and safer waters. All the passengers had gone to their berths and left me standing on the bog deck. While standing alone on the deck two women came from their berths, dressed only in sleeping robes. Each one of them took me by an arm, and for what reason I never knew, unless they suspected me of suicidal intentions. I declined their familiarity and they stepped back, but, as they afterwards told me, each one seized my coat-tail corners. While so standing the steamer struck a rock, known as "Yankee Rock," ran up on it, broke in two pieces, and all the stern sank instantly. I was pitched forward into the water and the two women with me, holding on to my coat-tail. I swam direct to shore, and the two women landed with me, holding their first grip upon my coat-tail. They told me that they could not swim, but they observed my motions and imitated me as nearly as they could by strokes and kicks. The accident occurred near Athens, and we were taken to the hotel and provided with dry cloths. I never saw the women after reaching the hotel. A great many people were drowned. I am not a spiritualist and hold no theory about the restraining hand or the two women. Living as I did a migratory life, without home or family ties, all of my effects were with me at the time I went aboard "The Swallow" for New York City. Everything in the way of baggage was lost, and I did not recover anything, fortunate to have saved my life when so many were drowned.

The above incident was narrated for this book, although I have never seen any account of it in print, nor have I heard it alluded to for fifty years.

Since referring to it, a friend has taken the trouble to search for the facts in history. The only record found is hereunto appended, and was taken from **The American Almanac** of 1846, page 340, containing the chronicles of events in 1845, in which record the incident is said to have occurred March 7, 1845, as follows:

"The Steamer 'Swallow,' on her passage from New York to Albany, was wrecked by running on an island in the evening, and the boat immediately breaking in two and the after-part sinking, a number of passengers were drowned."

The accompanying papers will show my residence in St. Louis between 1850-60:

CITY OF ST. LOUIS.

To all whom it may concern be it known

That G. E. D. Diamond, of the city of St. Louis, in the State of Missouri, having been nominated and confirmed, is by these presents appointed to be a private of the Night Guard for the city aforesaid.

To Have and to Hold said Appointment, and exercise the several duties, functions and franchises appertaining thereto, according to law, from the twelfth day of July, 1855, until the first Monday in June, 1856, unless sooner removed from office, or until his successor be duly appointed and qualified.

Given under my hand and the corporate seal of the said city, this twelfth day of July, A. D., 1855.

By the Mayor.

JOHN BRYAN, Registrar.

ST. LOUIS, Mo., March 13, 1858.

COL. CROPMANS

Dear Sir:—The bearer, Mr. G. E. D. Diamond, has been in my employ recently as Superintendent of Railroad Work, and as such has few equals; is faithful, sober and trustworthy, and for managing men and teams I think you cannot do better. I cordially would recommend him to your favorable notice.

Yours, etc., I. D. SMITH.

To Col. Cropman,
Deputy Quartermaster Gen., U. S. A.

MEN WHOM I HAVE KNOWN.

Referring to the men whom I have known, it is my privilege to name President James Monroe, for whom I cast my first vote for President of the United States in the year 1816. I am told that under a decision of one of our recent courts I could not have voted at that time, but in those days my first birthday was counted, and I was six months on my twenty-second year on the fourth of November, 1816.

Of the Boston men whom I knew were Lawrences, Nessmiths, Appletons, and others. For two and one-half years I was in the office of Benjamin Butler, Boston's bright attorney, trying to be a lawyer, but it did not work well in my case, so I gave it up.

An event occurred at that time to which I was an eye witness and General Butler was the actor. Judge Norcross was presiding judge, and General Butler was pleading a case at issue. A ruling of the judge very much displeased the lawyer, whereupon General Butler said:

"If your Honor will step down here, I will gladly show you a point in law which his Honor has never read, or if he has read it he does not understand it." His Honor accepted the invitation and came down from the bench to get a new point in law. When in front of the cock-eyed lawyer, Butler's right hand shot out and landed on his Honor's nose, felling him prostrate with bleeding nostrils. The first time Judge Norcross appeared in court after that—which was about two weeks—he was met at the bar by Butler who handed to him a large official envelope. The judge, supposing it to contain an apology, opened it, in the presence of the lawyers, with a flourish, when out and upon the floor fell a cartoon of his Honor as a jackass, and with it a pair of leather spectacles. A scramble followed by the lawyers for the spoils. One man got the goggles and another the jackass, whereupon the jackass was sold to the highest bidder, which was the man who had the leather goggles, for one hundred dollars, who exposed them in his office as an attraction to all comers.

Of St. Louis men I recall the names of Dr. McDonald, whose college was afterwards used for a prison; Dr. Adran, Dr. Shore, O. D. Finley, Henry T. Blow, Dr. Julian Bates, His Excellency John Howe, Mayor of the City; Governor Fletcher, Bob O. Blenness, who killed Brandt, and many others. I knew General Grant in St. Louis, first as a man hauling wood into the city, and later as a resident, moving into the city from the residence of his wife's father, Mr. Dent, where he remained until his own father took him from the city to Galena to learn how to tan hides, in which business he engaged from 1861 to 1865 very successfully. I personally knew General Siegel, General Harney, General Sterling Price, and a large list of men who became noted during the war, and have passed to the other side with the great majority.

I voted for every candidate on the Democratic ticket up to the election of General Wm. Henry Harrison in 1840, and for every Republican after the first election of Abraham Lincoln in 1860.

The most memorable campaign in which I ever engaged was in 1840, when Gen. Harrison was the candidate. At Albany, N. Y., of that year, I rode in the "Log Cabin," drawn by four hundred yoke of oxen, there being four lines of teams of one hundred yoke to the line, and we had "yokes of oxen to spare."

Fifty years later I marched in the line of Republicans in San Francisco who were "whooping it up" for the grandson, General Benjamin Harrison, then running for the Presidency of our country, at which time I was rounding out the first century of life.

So far as I know, all of the railroads on which I worked in those days have been rebuilt and changed to an up-to-date road. And all of the men with whom I had an acquaintance have passed away, and I am destined to be the last leaf on the tree in the spring.

EMPLOYED IN GOVERNMENT SERVICE.

As already indicated, I was in St. Louis engaged in building railroads when the war broke out in 1861. My acquaintance throughout the State of Missouri was very general, both with laboring men and officials of railroads. Because of my prejudice against signing away my liberty to come and go at pleasure, I did not enlist in the service as a soldier. The first conflict in Misouri after the war was declared was the taking of "Camp Jackson," situated three or four miles out of the city, in Lindell's pasture, which had been established by General Frost, who had gathered fresh recruits of Confederate sympathizers to the extent of about five to seven hundred.

Gen. Siegel, Gen. Lyons and Gen. Blair gathered up a corresponding number of Union sympathizers to go out and take the camp. I was of the number, because I could not see safety for our nation in any course except as a unit. There was no show for a fight at Camp Jackson, because every man skeddaddled who could get away, and we returned to the arsenal with three or four hundred prisoners.

"Chief Government Agent" was my official title from the opening to the end of the war, and my station was at St. Louis, in connection with the Quartermaster and Commissary Departments, General Robert Allen, Q. M. General. So far as I am aware, my judgment and action were never called in question by any superior in office.

The Transportation Department for the Western division of the army was under my special direction, as may be seen from the following correspondence, to-wit:

By telegram from Decatur.

Jan. 26, 1864.

TO CAPT. G. E. D. DIAMOND,

Chief Gov't Agent, St. Louis, Mo.:

Want transportation for eleven teamsters immediately.

6 Dp. Com. J. M. MOORE,

U. S. Military Telegraph.

Nov. 4, 1867.

TO CAPT. G. E. D. DIAMOND,
Gov't Agent, St. Louis.

Thirty-two (32) men arrived there at ten thirty (10:30) tonight. Wm. TATE.

Headquarters District of Missouri.

ST. LOUIS, April 5, 1864.

Special Order No. 88.

Samuel Lee and John Lee, Or. Master employes, will be released from Myrtle St. Prison and sent under guard to Capt.
G. E. D. Diamond, Chief Gov't Agt.

Capt, G. E. D. Diamond, I. P. Anderson.
Chief Gov't Agent. Provost Marshal.

Myrtle-Street Prison.

ST. LOUIS, April 5, 1864.

TO CAPT. G. E. D. DIAMOND,
Chief Gov't Agent.

Captain:—As per Special Order No. 88, I send you under guard the prisoners, Samuel Lee and Thomas, or John Lee.

I am, Captain, very respectfully,
Court of Prison. Your obedient servant,
B. KENDALL. J. M. McKELVY.

Headquarters Department of the Missouri.

ST. LOUIS, Sept. 7, 1864.

Captain:—The prisoner sent with this, Wm. Mont, is, by order of Brig. Gen'l James Lattens, sent to you. He was arrested several days ago for abusing the porters at their headquarters.

Very respectfully your obedient servant.
To Capt. Diamond, A. Q. M. Wm. Arthur.

Chief Engineer's Office.
U. S. Gun Boat.
ST. LOUIS, April 16, 1864.

TO CAPT. G. E. D. DIAMOND,
Chief Gov't Agent.

If you will discharge Wm. A. Swain from the Army, I shall then recommend him to the Hon. Secretary, of the Navy for an appointment as Acting 3d Assistant Engineer in one of the new gun boats. Respectfully,

Your obedient servant,

J. W. KING.
Chief Engineer, U. S. Navy.

Capt. G. E. D. Diamond,
Chief Gov't Agent, St. Louis, Mo.

Office of the Chief Quartermaster,
Department of the Misouri.

To the Honorable Judge of the Law Commission Court, St. Louis, Mo.

Sir:—The services of the bearer, G. E. D. Diamond, being indispensably necessary for the conduct of the public business of this department, I respectfully request that he be excused from serving on juries.

Yours very respectfully,
Your servant,
W. MYER, A. Q. M.

The above documents have been selected from scores of others which I have kept in my possession, and I now use them as evidence of my official relation to the Government during the war.

I kept all of my own accounts, and I now recall an occasion when one official asked me for a report in the course of the next six months. The same afternoon I handed to him the desired report from my books, which surprised him as much as if I had attached wings to his shoulders and sent him home by air line. I herewith append a copy of the report which he desired within six months:

Quartermaster's Department,
Office of Transportation.
ST. LOUIS, Mo., Jan. 15, 1863.

CAPT. DIAMOND, General Agent.

Dear Sir:—Will you please report to me the number of men transported to St. Louis on each of the following passes, viz:

Pass No. 86,254, May 30, 1863.
Pass No. 86,291, June 11, 1863.
Pass No. 86,293, June 11, 1863.
Pass No. 86,252, May 30, 1863.

Very respectfully,
L. DWIGHT EATON,
Supt. R. R. Trans.

I have cherished for many years the high compliments paid me during the war by General Grant, for my accuracy in managing transportation of men and material with dispatch and promptness. When he landed in San Francisco from his trip around the world, in 1881, he treated me with deference and urged me to accept a trip in company with his suite to Washington City, out of respect for kindness shown him before the war, when he was noted more for obscurity than for greatness. General Grant was naturally a good and meek man, the first principles of true greatness.

MY EXPERIENCE IN ST. LOUIS.

After the war, I remained in St. Louis until 1873. Immediately after the war I engaged with Porter & Wolfe, in real estate, collection of rents and so forth. Leaving them I engaged in the same line of business in my own name, until I again resumed work upon railroads. My first railroad work after the war was upon the Lexington and Sedalia, from Lexington to Sedalia, of which employment I have no record at hand.

The following shows my presence in St. Louis in 1868, and is the only document I have in hand covering the time from the end of the war until my emigration to Oregon in 1873.

"THIS AGREEMENT, entered into on this, the 3d day of October, A. D., 1868, between Wm. E. Plant and G. E. D. Diamond, both of the city of St. Louis, Mo., witnesseth.

"That the said Wm. E. Plant, as general Western agent of the Florence Sewing Machine Company, hereby agrees to pay the said G. E. D. Diamond one of the Extra Cabinet Closed, No. 10, Rosewood, Polished, Sewing Machines, of the value of $175, and the sum of $50 in cash, for the services of the said Diamond for six days, at the Agricultural and Mechanical Fair of St. Louis, commencing Monday, October 5, and closing Saturday, October 10, in showing and representing the interest of the Florence Sewing Machines, and in distributing bills and cards advertising the same upon the Fair Grounds.

"The said Plant further agrees to pay the said Diamond the sum of $5 for each and every sewing machine sold by the said Diamond.

"Witness our hands and seals, this, the 3d day of October, A. D., 1868.

Wm. E. PLANT. (Seal)
G. E. D. DIAMOND. (Seal)

In the year 1873 I started for the Pacific Coast with two teams and two men, leading some stock. On the way I fell in with one hundred and four emigrant wagons. Every woman in the company was attacked with mountain fever, but the men escaped. I carried with me some medicines and some olive oil and directions how to use them, which proved very successful in the cases of mountain fever and won for myself the title of "Dr," but being a "mountain" doctor the title left me when I reached the plains.

Leaving St. Louis, we came by way of Kansas City, Cheyenne, Silver City, Boise and John Day Valley, striking Oregon at Lebanon, thence to Salem, where I engaged in the delivery of wheat to the water for shipment. From Salem to Portland, and thence to Astoria, at which place I was engaged in the canneries with Joseph Humes, also with Captain Flavelle on the wharf. On the first day of January, 1877, I landed in San Francisco off the George W. Elder, on her first trip to the Pacific Coast, at which time I was eighty years and eight months old.

My first employment in San Francisco was with Charles Crocker, as guard on the grounds of his new building, then in progress of construction on California street, and my next engagement was with Thomas Williams, owner of the Kidd Ranch on Union Island, in the Construction of a canal one mile long, connecting "Old River" with "Middle River," in which employment I was engaged about one year, leaving after being filled chock full of malaria, which I threw off as quickly as possible here in San Francisco.

My next business employment was with Mr. Casebolt, of the Sutter-street Car Line, and my duty was in charge of a dummy, a position now known as gripman. Everything went along all right until a reporter for the Evening Post took occasion to say in the Post that Mr. Casebolt kept a man in his employ (running a dummy) who was eighty-three years old. Mr. Casebolt showed considerable interest in the report, lest the public might think him negligent of their welfare by entrusting the lives of the people to a man in his dotage.

One day an accident occurred on the road to one of the cars and Mr. Casebolt hastened to the scene, walking straight up to the man in charge of the car, and seeing signs of frost gathering about his head and face, charged him with being eighty-three years old. The man felt himself greatly insulted, and squared off to a set-to to convince his employer that he was not yet superannuated. The man proved to be about forty-five years old. Not long after that another accident occurred, and Mr. Casebolt again charged a man, yet on the sunny side of fifty, of being eighty-three years old. The manager of the road fared worse this time than in the former case, and resolved to tackle the reporter for the evidence of his statements. The reporter was seen, who maintained his position, saying to Mr. Casebolt that he could prove that he had a man in his employ, in charge of a dummy, who was eighty-three years old, and that his name was Diamond.

The cat was out of the bag then, and Mr. Casebolt came direct to me with the heavy charge of being an old man. Then it was my time to get hot, for I did not enjoy being called old in those days any more than I do now. I replied by saying: "Well, what of it, if I am a hundred years old? Have I not done my work well? Has my car met with an accident? Go look after those young fellows who meet with accidents." He turned away without expressing an opinion, but I expected a long furlough. Instead of that he came to me and asked if I could take two cars to the terminus of the line, near the Occidental Hotel, and bring them out full of "High School Girls?" My reply was, "I can take fourteen cars and bring out as many girls as the cable can haul if you will furnish the cars and the girls." He assigned me to the dummy of a young man, and I carried down two cars, and hauled out both of them loaded with "High School Girls."

At the crossing of Larkin and Sutter streets we were halted, where the girls in the cars, the "eighty-three-year-old man" and the "High School Girls" were photographed. I here offer a generous reward for one of those pictures, having loaned my copy to a friend who forgot to return it. It is altogether probable that I would not know many of those girls if I should meet them, because it is possible that they have changed a little since that time.

Not long after that I learned that the Occidental Hotel wanted an engineer, so I applied for the position. Mr. Charles Wetherbee was then manager, whose attention I called to the fact that at one time I was the guest of his uncle, Deacon Wetherbee, of Lowell, Mass., for several years in succession. Mr. Wetherbee expressed regret that he had just engaged a man for engineer, and offered me the position of night watchman, with the refusal of engineer if the man employed did not suit. I accepted the offer and remained in the hotel in that capacity for seven and one-half years, when Mr. Wetherbee retired, and after that one year with his successor, Mr. Arnold.

From there I went to the Baldwin hotel in the same capacity with increased wages, $10, where I remained for four and one-half years, bringing the time down to about 1893, and my age up to about ninety-seven years. During the thirteen years with both hotels I never lost an hour from any cause, nor did any accident occur under my care. Since that time I have been steadily engaged in the selling of books, such as the "Encyclopedies," "Standard Dictionary," "Redpath's History," and other large books, carrying them from place to place, and walking from ten to twenty-five miles a day,

My evenings are very generally taken by old friends who drop in to talk, or by strangers who know me, and desire to know how I manage to survive a century and enjoy the world in health and happiness.

I tell them, as I tell you, dear readers, that I enjoy every hour of my life. I am ready for this life or the life to come and have no choice which shall have claims upon me tomorrow. I believe that this life is preparatory, and that I shall live again, or rather that I shall never die, only be changed from one state into another from the lower to the higher.

CORRESPONDENCE.

SAN FRANCISCO, Feb. 14, 1888.

To His Excellency,

BENJAMIN HARRISON,

President of the United States:

My Dear General:—My principal object in addressing you at this time is to congratulate you on being the choice of our great nation as its Chief Magistrate.

As the voice of our State has expressed its choice for you, I, as a private individual, but no less your friend, desire to extend to you a most cordial invitation, in behalf of the whole people, to come out to our Coast, for we would be glad to see you and shake hands with the grandson of that good and great man, William Henry Harrison, whose acquaintance and friendship I had the privilege and honor to enjoy in 1840, and for whom, of course, I voted.

With profound respect for you, and sincerely wishing you a prosperous and a successful adminstration, I remain,

Your friend and obedient servant,

G. E. D. DIAMOND,

San Francisco, Cal.

(Age 92, May 1, 1888.)

BENJAMIN HARRISON,
274 North Delaware Street,
INDIANAPOLIS, Ind., Feb. 22, 1888.
G. E. D. DIAMOND, Esq.,
San Francisco, Cal.

My Dear Sir:—I am in receipt of your letter of the 18th inst., and beg to thank you for your kind congratulations and expressions of good will.

Very truly yours,
BENJ. HARRISON.

RECAPITULATION.

My effort has been to furnish the evidence of my existence for one hundred and two years, and although I do not possess papers complete of the advancing years, yet I feel that I have furnished data sufficiently correct and united to complete a chain of links one hundred and two years long.

First. The records of Plymouth, Mass., will show that the Diamonds resided there in May, 1796.

Second. The records of Oxford County, State of Maine, will show the same Diamonds there from the year of my birth and until after the war of 1812.

Third. The details of my life, after leaving my father's house, have been set forth with sufficient accuracy to admit of being traced until 1852, when I was attacked with yellow fever. To escape from that district I have named the two boats which carried me, one to New Orleans and the other to Cincinnati, and the name of the hotel where I stopped in the latter place. Those ships have a history, and their presence there at that time can be ascertained with as much accuracy as the astronomers can tell the whereabouts of the planets at that time.

Fourth. My papers show my presence in St. Louis in 1855 and 1858, and no doubt that the city records as well as the books of the railroad companies will show my presence and my employment up to 1861, when the war began.

Fifth. My war record is too extensive to admit of any doubt. If any one is still in doubt on that score it will be a pleasure to me to exhibit to him more papers in evidence than he will care to read. The years following the war I was in St. Louis and the city records, books of business firms, and other method of proof, with the accompanied agreement in 1868 will support my statement about my presence in St. Louis from the close of the war until I left for the Pacific Coast.

Sixth. My presence in Oregon as already detailed, naming places where men with whom I was employed ought to show clearly of my presence in that State. My California presence on the first day of January, 1877, is linked with the first arrival of the Geo. W. Elder, and her history is written. Each place of employment named by me, together with the names of men and business firms, companies and so forth, supported by the city directories with my address from year to year, and all supported by men here and living leaves my Pacific Coast record without question.

SIGNS OF INFIRMITY AND HOW ARRESTED.

To me sickness was an alien all through the morning of life. Not until I was nearly twenty years old did I meet with his enemy of the flesh. At that time I had what was known as the black measels, in its worst form. The result of this sickness was impaired sight and hearing. Hoping that time would restore my afflicted senses no attention was given to them for three or four years.

After three years my eyes were very painful, water running from them and a film gathering over them. My hearing was quite dull and growing worse. The feeling that my two most important senses were failing me caused most painful sensations of profound grief. Not being familiar with the science of medicine and so unused to the services of a physician, I did not look in that direction for a remedy. I made it a subject of intense thought. I recalled the deep interest I had taken in the reading of the Hebrew Kings, how they were annointed with olive oil, and how olive oil was used as a means of healing and physical preservation.

After deliberate consideration I resolved to resort to the use of the best olive oil I could get for an external application. I was then in the State of New York. After securing pure olive oil, for which I paid $8.00 a quart, I applied it first to the eyes, rubbing the oil upon the eyelids, beneath the eye and under the lids of the eyes. But two or three months' applications were made before decided improvements appeared. The sore place healed, stiff places became flexible, water ceased to flow so profusely, and the film less troublesome.

I had granulated eyelids which I cured solely by the use of pure olive oil.

The change was so great that I resolved to use oil for the loss of hearing. I used oil freely about the ears externally, and put drops of oil into the ears, holding it there with bits of cotton balls. In a very short time my sight and hearing were entirely restored. I did not leave off treating them because they appeared to be free from infirmity, but have kept them well oiled for sixty years, and they have never failed me whenever called into service.

Not until I was past three score years did I again feel the effects of infirmity. At that time I was in St. Louis, engaged in railroad construction. Up to that time I had never felt signs of rigidity of bones or joints, and knew not that the machinery was running down. One day I jumped from a wagon to the ground and my joints did not respond with the usual rebound. I was startled and surprised. Resuming my place in the wagon I leaped to the ground again, as a proof trial. The proof was there, for not only did the knees refuse to rebound, but the backbone creaked and cried out in pain. I was humiliated and gave way to tears and general lamentations. Self-preservation is the first law of nature, and my senses at once sought for a remedy. The cure of failing sight and hearing by the use of oil externally, led me to believe that the same remedy might apply to hardening bones and rigid joints.

Looking at the wagon from which I jumped, it occurred to me that when the wheels dragged heavily on the spindles we oiled the spindles; that when any machine creaked we sought the noisy part and applied lubricating oil. Acting on the principle suggested by such reasoning, I resolved to begin the practice of oiling every joint and such portions of the physical frame as might be subject to rigid and hardening processes of old age.

I took into consideration the fact that I belonged to a family of long-lived people. It was not because I desired extreme long life, but for the reason that I wished to enjoy life as long as it lasted, that caused me to enter upon a special care of the body.

Although I had lived a temperate life, I had not made a study of the kind and quantity of food required for comfort and longevity. By observation and reading it came to me that it is possible to prevent or arrest the age of decline and keep the joints flexible and the bodily organs sound to the end of a reasonably long life.

My age at that time was about sixty-five years, and my appearance as represented by the photograph in the front of this book. The two things, as it appeared to me, required to attain the results which I desired, were diet and oil. To carry out my plan I knew that self-mastery was the chief obstacle to overcome. By this I mean, that personal attention must be given to the body and that the palate must be educated to self-denial and correct taste.

HOW I USED OIL.

Having secured such oil as to me was the best, I began by first preparing the skin to receive it. To this end the ordinary plunge bath, or tub bath, was discarded, and the sponge bath system put into practice. Nor did I find it desirable to use warm water, but resorted to cold or tepid water. I use a wet and soaped towel, which I pass over the body, rubbing every part as thoroughly and as rapidly as possible. Rinsing the towel as dry as possible apply it again thoroughly, finishing with a course, dry towel. After that I use a course brush upon the skin until the blood is out to the surface and rushing through the body rapidly. Now the system is ready to absorb the oil, and apply it where it can be the most useful.

Turning a little oil into the hallow of the hand I apply it to the joints, on the inside especially,—that is, under the arms, in elbows, in rear of knees, on the insteps and in the groins. After that upon the shoulders, spine, hips knees, bottom of feet, and frequently on top of the head. Rub with the hands until the oil is absorbed and nothing on the surface to show upon the most delicate fabric. Off to bed and the oil is preparing the machine for hard work tomorrow.

This practice I began and have kept it up, sometimes both morning and evening, for the past sixty years for the eyes and ears, and nearly forty years for the bones and joints. This treatment should not seem a strange thing to any one. The gardener knows he must enrich the soil if he continues to gather produce from it. This body is made of dust and is soil and requires an enriching just as its mother.

But the reader will say, "that is a great deal of trouble." Certainly! There are many who think that they can have health by praying for it. Prayer is not availing where the use of common sense is not applied. Time preys upon the body, but the man cannot prevent it by praying. Nature tells us to live a temperate life and use the means which common sense knows is within reach and offer their services for the using.

WHAT I EAT AND DRINK.

Long life and good health are not sustained alone by external applications. That which enters within a man tells the story of building up and pulling down.

Breathing, eating, drinking are the three processes of taking into the body the vital forces of nature. These forces work outward and afford something to be washed, rubbed and oiled. Three things I have faithfully practiced in the past half century, jointly. The first is that of breathing the freshest air possible, long, deep draughts. The second is the selection and eating of the best bone and blood food at my command. The third is the use of pure water at proper time and temperature. When I began to prepare the body for long and healthy life, I left out of my diet slaughtered meats. Strong meat, often taken, is the source of all kinds of disease, laying the foundation for untold suffering.

MY DAILY MENU.

BREAKFAST—
Cup of hot water,
Whole wheat or barley mush and milk,
Boiled codfish with potatoes,
Whole wheat, health bread and olive oil,
Two poached eggs,
Apple sauce,
Fruit in season.

LUNCHEON—
Fruit.

DINNER—
Hot water,
Vegetable or rice-tomato soup,
Whole wheat bread, buttered or with olive oil,
Sweet potatoes,
Beans,
Hot milk,
Fruit in season.

Meals varied with corresponding diet. Never use white bread. It is absolutely worthless.

OLIVE OIL.

The reader will observe that I have not specified the kinds of oil I use. There are many kinds of oil—animal oil and vegetable oil. Animal oil I have used, but only as a necessary substitute. The best of the animal oils for my use are the pickerel oil, goose oil and skunk's grease, which I would use if necessity required. When I resolved to make use of oil as a means of preservation, and after thorough testing, I settled upon OLIVE OIL, first press. My experience has been that imported olive oil is not pure. Impure olive oil means cotton seed oil, and is dangerous to use; nor is it safe as a condiment or medicine. A part of it is a gum. It will not digest nor will it burn. Imported olive oil is a dangerous oil to use. I am not selling nor handling any kind of olive oil, foreign or domestic. I have sampled every brand of California olive oil, so far as I know. IT IS NOT ALL PURE. Imported olive oil is a dangerous cotton seed oil adulteration. To be sure there are grades of our domestic olive oil known as "first and second pressing" and their quality and value are in the order as above named. For my purposes, which I designate as medicinal, the best is the only kind I use. It has been suggested to me that olive oil is expensive, and that bathing in it is beyond the reach of the average man. I do not bathe in oil. The amount I use upon each occasion will not exceed a tablespoonful. Sufficient is enough of anything, and in the practice each one will soon discover the quantity he desires to use as an ointment, condiment or medicine.

Born in Massachusetts, reared in the province which is Maine, lived in New York, Florida, Alabama, Mississippi and Missouri; crossed the plains through Kansas, Nebraska, Wyoming, Montana and into Oregon; and for thirty years last past a resident of California, I am free to say that no man ever lived who is deserving of better things than California produces and so generously bestows upon him, among which is pure olive oil.

SELECTION OF FOOD AND DRINK.

The selection of food and drink is of vast importance in youth, but it does not become of first importance in the estimation of men until they have reached the meridian of life. By this time the machinery of the physical man has been running several decades with but little attention, and there is rheumatism, chronic headache, liver pains, kidney troubles, stomach rebellions, dyspepsia, which means chronic constipation. It is generally known and admitted by the most thoughtful people that by far the greater amount of physical suffering is the result of eating too much or eating the wrong kind of food. A man will be systematic in allowancing his horse to two quarts of oats, and is careful to confine him so that he cannot get to the oat bin and eat all he wants lest he "founder" on every little provocation. The same man will go from the stable to the table and sit down to eat of at least ten varieties of food, the most of it cooked in poor oil fats, and during the meal drink freely of water, wine and coffee, capping it off with a cigar.

That man will get into his road-wagon, behind that scientifically fed horse, and reel off ten miles an hour. When he gets there his horse is in good condition, but he walks up the lawn slope of two hundred yards, holding his stomach with both hands and panting like a fat ox. He is a crank on horse feeding and a fool about feeding himself.

If it is good to measure out oats to a horse, is it not better to weigh out food for a man? Good, scientific judgment argues that the maximum supply for man is seven pounds per day —about one-fourth of solids and three-fourths of fluid.

The exact quantity and quality of food for a man is governed very much by active and climatic conditions, as well as by the period in one's life when taken. Good, common sense would not weigh out the same food to a man in his study as to a man who follows the plow or wields the ax. Nor would good sense weigh out the same quantity and quality of food to the same man in the torrid zone which had been weighed out to him in the frigid zone. And what brings it nearer to our countrymen is this: that a clear head will not send into the stomach the same food in the hot months of July and August that was given in the ten-degrees-below-zero months of January and February. What is still more an unreasonable proposition is that a man should be so thoughtless as to force upon his system as much and as strong food at the age of fifty, sixty and seventy, as when twenty, thirty and forty years old.

The exact noon-time of life is not always the same in all people. When development ceases and decline begins is a thing of experience. How to treat the body to prevent decline, and how to arrest rigidity, after it has set in, are important things to note in life.

The ingenuity of man has been tested to its utmost to devise ways and means to prevent the decay and decline of wood and metals in machinery, and to arrest the progress of weakening by time and elements. No less interest has been taken in man by true scientific thinkers, who have written books and delivered lectures, but the great mass of mankind have gone on plunging after the almighty dollar, searching for pleasure or climbing for fame, refusing to think and provide against the ravages of time and ward off the insidious calcareous matter which is making inroads upon the bones and joints of their physique. By reference to the four photographs, pages 3, 39 and 47 of this book, one taken at the age of sixty-five, another at the age of one hundred years, and the third at almost one hundred and two years, and one at one hundred and five years, the reader will see the same man at the earlier age showing signs of decline and rigidity and the other pictures, thirty-five to forty years later, presenting evidence of an arrest of decline and the turning back of the hands of time. It is a well known fact that the mission of the blood circulating through the system is to carry supplies to the several vital organs. Now, if the fluids and solids in the period of life attained, the result must be ill to the body. To prevent ossification the calcerous earthly matter must be restricted at the entrance door to the body, by refusing it admission through the food and drink which supply the system. These two, solids and fluids, are the sources of calcareous earthly matter which enter into the blood and are finally deposited in all the tissues, membranes, vessels and solids of the body producing "old age" as shown by the bones, joints and general decrepitude, as rigidity proceeds and claims its victim.

But the inquiry arises what are the foods and fluids containing a dangerous amount of calcareous earthly matters. The greater portion of the body, is fluid. The question of what shall I drink? is of untold importance. The fluid enters more directly into the blood and carries with it the quality of its composition. Water is not the same quality in all places. What is known as spring or well water is laden with the enemy of the physical being. Water of an average quality is composed of carbonates and lime in such quantities that by constant use up to the middle life a man has taken into his system enough calcareous matter to form a pillar of solid chalk, marble or salt, not unlike Lot's wife after she looked back.

The reader may wonder how one manages to live even to middle life. Were it not that the kidneys and other secreting organs stand at their post of duty, day and night, throwing off such injurious matter, a man would be old at twenty-five. These organs cannot throw off all of this foreign foe, because it escapes into other portions of the body a little every day. In the course of time this solid matter becomes general in the system, turns on the screws, rivets the nails, tightens the joints, destroys elasticity, and brings on the era of rigidity. And, madam, you tell me that you did not know of the character of our common everyday spring and well water? I think you are mistaken. Every woman who has charge of the cooking vessel knows how difficult it is to scrape off the deposit on the bottom of the kettle in which water has boiled. That is lime deposit which went into the kettle as water, and settled upon the bottom of the kettle a strong white solid. How much of that deposit upon the membraneous lining of the stomach do you think human life can stand? How much of it distributed here and there by the blood into the various organs of the body would it take to do up a strong system? Do you repeat your question of from whence comes this calcareous matter which deposits chalk and lime in the body producing rigidity and old age?

The body is a garrison. Within are the sentinels on guard, armed and equipped to resist an enemy of certain strength. When the enemy becomes stronger than the armed sentinels within, the garrison surrenders. Even when in good health a struggle is going on within the body between a two-inch supply and too-little removal. The power to remove or throw off these accummulations diminish with age, and unless the amount taken into the body is lessened, the sense of heaviness and stiffness is felt which is approaching old age.

That one may extend life and enjoy it free from decrepitude and constant suffering, what must be done? An effort must be made to prevent salts, which are held in solution by water, from becoming a deposit in the body. The process is as simple as filling and emptying a reservoir. It the pipe which conveys water to the reservoir is two-inch, and the exit pipe is but one and one-half inch, it is evident that it is only a question of time when the reservoir will overflow. It is so with the body. When the supply becomes excessive and the resisting power weakens with age, the deposits increase and the body is forced into voluntary bankruptcy. This is termed: "growing old," "infirmity of old age," "rigidity," and "ossification," all of which terms mean "off to the bone yard"

Can this condition of life be resisted? Can one so order his food and drink as to ward off the infirmities of old age? Is there a time when decline and decay may be arrested and the bodily organs continued in business at the old stand?

The answer to this question is a thing of experience with me. I know this is possible and that it has occurred in my case. Every thoughful mind given to attain this end can solve this problem by using onlv such food and drink as will keep the body elastic and free from pain. Nature has sentinels at every gate of exit, warning the commandant of the post that danger threatens the citadel. The names of some of the sentinels are "Rheumatism," "Piles," "Constipation," "Colds," "Neuralagia," "Cramps," "Side Pains," "Appendicitis," etc., etc. If the waste pipe becomes clogged with sediment, and the pressure is not relieved, the pipe bursts. So great is the waste of the body through the pores, that if these visible apertures were closed for an hour suffering is certain. A child was once painted to imitate a bronze figure, and through ignorance of the managers the paint was left on the child too long, resulting in sudden death.

Harken to the voice of these sentinels which nature has placed at the outer stations of the physique, and then warn the too highly educated palate that taste cannot be gratified at the expense of so much suffering, limited usefulness and short life.

The only complaint against Dives is that he had too much to eat and wore too fine linen, and so he wanted Lazarus sent back to this world to tell his brothers not to eat so much nor to wear such fine clothes. There are better uses to which to put cash, food and raiment than to overfeed and clothe the body, cut short the life and fail to enjoy this world. The man who sins against his own body sins against his neighbor, against nature and against his Maker.

My rule is to avoid cold ice water, and not to drink unboiled water unless it be distilled. Nature intended that man should live on the products of the earth. To provide for his thirst, nature draws up the water from the rivers and the rills, distills it, sends it down into the earth and up through the roots of vegetation, into the leaves and bark, fruit and nuts, and in such proportions as to provide for hunger and thirst in nature's own gifts. Even dried fruits can be restored to their original quality by the free use of distilled water. But men tell me that they thirst and must take large quantities of water to satisfy that thirst. Certainly! But they are large meat eaters, not because of the meat they have taken; or perhaps they are accustomed to the use of stimulants and narcotics, introducing foreign elements into the body, thus reserving nature. As the jaded horse submits to the lash, so the exhausted energies of man resort to stimulants. The body seeks to obey nature in rest, but the ambitious man urges on by the use of strong coffee, wine, beer or liquid until nature is exhausted.

The man who thinks well of his body will study how much nature can endure, as the architect studies the weight of the superstructure before he selects the size and material for supports. The thin man can put on flesh and the fat man can put it off. At the age of ninety-three years I weighed 225 pounds, with but five feet seven inches height, for two successive summers I went into the hot climate of California, lived on fruits, nuts and melons mainly, and dropped to 142 1-2 pounds, since which time I have not gone above 160 pounds. The thin man can fatten his cattle and hogs, why cannot he put flesh upon his own skeleton? I have never used the pipe, cigar or cigarette; never indulged in wine, liquors, nor any stimulants, omitting entirely the use of tea and coffee. None of these things contain food, and nature rebels at their use until through custom or social life the taste is educated to indulge in them, after which nature receives them because too weak to resist an encroaching enemy.

My practice is such as comes within the reach of the common people. The working man and woman can ward off disease, suffering and premature death by the use of these means, and enjoy life to a ripe old age.

My practice and advice is not attractive to the man who has "money to burn" and passions to serve as a master. The after-dinner man, the banquet man, the rich clubman and the high-tea ladies may not be interested in these simple methods of living long and living happily, because they prefer the good things of today, and let the morrow come with its heavy bills, in the shape of pains, aches and early death. The rich man who fares sumptuously, is ill, peevish, goutish and miserable, but his valet nurses, cares for and ministers unto him, feeding himself upon the crumbs from the rich man's table.

THE SERMON MAKER.

It was late one Saturday evening when a well-dressed and easy mannered man rang my door bell and was admitted. He proved to be a minister, and I sized him up as already having one sermon ready, and was looking for material for an off-hand evening talk. He began by referring to my advanced years, and expressed a wish to know my views upon the subject of Christianity. My first response was that I regarded Christianity a good thing to live by, but I did not see very much of it in practice.

"Have you carefully investigated the Bible?"

"I have read it through ten times besides the re-readings."

"Do you not believe it is the veritable Word of God?"

"Assuming that there is a God, it is a reasonable proposition that He may have inspired this book."

"But you speak of God as a being assumed and not real. Do I understand you?"

"You understand me as well as I understand the preachers and theological teachers. Those brainy men differ so widely that I think they must assume a good deal."

"But does not the Bible teach the highest and best morals and the fairest system of man's obligation to his fellow man?"

"That was one question which worried me in reading about the extermination of the original owners of Caanan, neither sparing old nor young."

"Yes, my friend, but it is within your recollection that the Indians have been exterminated to make way for a higher order of men and governments."

"I do recall that when the Government wished to send the Indians west from Maine, the Maine men said No, but we will keep them, treat them right, and make good citizens of them. So they did, and they became models of industry and citizenship. Indian barbarism seems to have increased on the borders of our Christian civilization."

"Still, you recognize that our up-to-date nations are the highest forms of civilization yet known, do you not?"

"It occurs to me that our up-to-date civilization is a failure in some respects, and especially in this, that it has failed to restrain the strong and protect the weak, which was the principal doctrine of the Great Teacher of Nazareth."

"I am glad to hear you recognize the Master, the Great Teacher of Nazareth. Do you not believe that He was the son of God?"

"Now, my ministerial friend, you are pushing my little barque a long way from shore. If I could comprehend God I might form an opinion of his creative power. The greatest being or thing not of earth of which I have certain knowledge is the sun, without which everything of life would be chaos and death. If the heavens declare the glory of God, and He made the sun, moon and stars, then I believe in His Almighty power, power sufficient to create all things out of nothing; to incarnate Himself in our flesh; to become like us in form but infinitely superior to us in wisdom and dominion, able to make a sacrifice of Himself or His Son, sufficient to redeem worlds of humanity."

"One more question, my veteran friend. Do you believe that if ever you should leave this earth that you will live again?"

"Yes! I believe that! I believe that the spirit of man never dies. I shall live again, and trust to a Saving Power which I recognize but cannot comprehend.

"Good night!"

"Good night, and come again."

Exit minister.

FRATERNAL ASSOCIATION.

My life has been both single and singular, in this, that I never married nor joined a fraternity, except as an honorary member of a society of which the "lone pine tree" is a symbol.

State of Maine Association
of California.

OAKLAND, Cal., July 25, 1896.

Capt. G. E. D. DIAMOND,
San Francisco, Cal.

Dear Sir:—We take great pleasure in informing you that, at a meeting held June 11,

1896, you were elected an honorary member of the State of Maine Association of California.

The pamphlet herewith enclosed, to which your attention is kindly asked, fully sets forth the objects of the Association.

Trusting that our action will meet with your approval, and indulging the hope that we may have the pleasure of greeting you at some future reunion of our Association,

We are, very truly, yours,

D. H. HASKELL,
President.

FRED A. POOR, Secretary.
By W. G. Dinsmore, Vice-President.

From "Nineteenth Annual Reunion," 1896:

"One of the pleasing incidents of the occasion was the presence with us of Capt. G. E. D. Diamond, formerly of Maine. Capt. Diamond has passed his one hundredth natal anniversary, and there are no apparent physical reasons why he will not be able to meet us at many future reunions; he was made an honorary member of the Association at this meeting. An adherence to the temperate habits formed in Maine, stimulated by OUR 'glorious climate,' guarantees good health as well as length of years."

Thanks are due, and hereby tendered, the "State of Maine Association" for their kindly recognition. Long live the State of Maine Association.

SECOND EDITION.

Dr. A. E. Osborne, who had charge of the Institute of Feeble-Minded Children, at Glen Ellen, has declared that pure olive oil as a food has no rival. He has given the results of his experiments in treating diseases. I will here insert a few of them:

No. 1. Two years ago measels swept through the institution. Over sixty patients were down at the same time. As a rule in this disease there is considerable nausea and a sense of dryness and of pain until the eruption is fully "out." Then, during the eruption, unless special measures be taken to prevent, a draught may produce a chill, causing the eruption to "go in," and followed, perhaps, by congestion of the lungs, or of the kidneys, or of both. Most of the fatal cases terminate in this way. The thirst is always severe, and the danger to the eyesight and hearing following continued congestion very considerable and annoying. Lacking the proper hospital facilities, I recognized that my patients were most unfavorably situated, as we were obliged to treat them in the regular sleeping dormitories, just as they happened to be taken. My invariable treatment was to take them as fast as they showed signs of the disease, give them a thorough hot water sponging from head to foot, followed immediately, and repeated at intervals of every few hours with copious inunctions of warm olive oil, well rubbed in. Mucilaginous drinks and a generous diet completed the treatment. According to the amount of oil used there was absence of the persistent thirst; the eruptions "came out" several hours earlier than is usual, afforded no particular sense of pain, and was attended with no undue congestion. All recovered nicely, notwithstanding the extreme delicate condition of many previously. The mainstay of the treatment was the oil (no drugs being used), and its application was repeated ad libitum day and night. Whenever the skin became dry and hot the oil relieved it and brought to the patient a sense of relief, surely followed by sleep, from which they awoke refreshed. In scarlet fever the frequent inunctions of hot olive oil are peculiarly effective in sustaining the patient and obviating many dangerous complications. From personal trials, details of which would be tedious here, I am convinced that of any single remedy in this disease, olive oil is the most valuable and potent —which, I am aware, is saying a great deal, and more than I expect will be believed by any one unfamiliar with its virtues.

No. 2. Case of an idio-imbecile boy, six years old; contracted pneumonia; both lungs involved, and disease stubborn from onset. Previous history bad, a strong syphilitic taint being well rooted in a scrofulous constitution. Owing to individual idiosyncrasies, diet previously had been limited to bread and milk and a little of well-cooked potato; digestion and power of assimilation correspondingly poor. In addition to usual treatment, gave olive oil internally on bread, and well salted, and externally, to body and limbs, by hand-rubbing, afterwards followed by wrapping in oiled cloths. He recovered from the pneumonia. Other tests have demonstrated the superiority of olive oil over cod liver oil in consumption, which, again, I am aware is saying a great deal with a few strokes of the pen. Cod liver oil disgusts the palate, clogs the stomach, overtaxes the digestive juices to emulcify it, and lastly, is again an animal product, generally of filthy manufacture, and so adulterated with chemical "what nots," under various sophistries, that we say with a meaning, "God help the wretch who takes the ordinary article as it is found in the market."

No. 3 High grade imbecile youth, of eighteen years of age. Has a malarious history, and for some years has shown signs of passive hyperaemia of the liver. Appetite very capricious, and diet correspondingly self-limited. Under no circumstances whatever can he be prevailed upon to take fruit in any form. Two months ago he began to walk stiffly, complexion rapidly assumed a dirty, coffee-ground color, particularly in patches. Complained of pain in the limbs, particularly the knee joints. On examination, had, nodulous swellings were discovered on knees and on shin bones, afterward appearing erratically on back, arms and ankles. In a short time almost any movement caused him distress, and I detected hallucinations of sight and hearing. Altogether, it made a remarkably interesting case, with recovery doubtful. Emaciation was rapid and pronounced. Medication with medicines proper was of little avail, so I fell back upon the use of olive oil, hoping that if only as a nutrient it would afford some relief. I did not expect a cure. I had the fellow oil-massaged from head to foot, twice or more a day, and then rolled in blankets, literally reeking in oil, and kept warm. Long and refreshing sleeps followed; then came increased movements of the limbs. All medicines were finally withheld, and the oil alone persevered in. The nodules slowly disappeared; the skin began to clear; in a week or so he could wriggle out of bed, became gradually more and more cheerful in mind, and at the expiration of a week he could stand on his feet sufficiently long for the attendant to rub him down; then his appetite improved, and considerable nourishment was taken with apparent relish. All pain left him; he began to take on flesh, steadily improved, and is now preparing to take a trip home to the southern part of the State. Although, practically, fully recovered, he has a slight oil massage every night on retiring. The most significant fact about the case is that the biliary secretions seemed to be immediately influenced by the oil, and that the urine, which in the beginning indicated kidney complaint cleared up at once.

During the last seventy-five years of my life I used gallons of olive oil. One-half cup three to five times a day, on an empty stomach cure for stomach trouble, indigestion, tapeworm, complete; gravel, concretions in the kidneys, stiff joints, pimples on the skin, scrofula (a disease affecting the glands, especially of the neck), and fevers, severe pains in the region of the kidneys, painful urination, and in the widest range of cases, and with the happiest results. It is kept handy for all sorts of use and in every truth a household remedy. Leaving out of consideration its laxative properties as before enumerated, my experience warrants me in giving it precedence as a reconstructive and to assume the following conclusions:

First.—It stands unrivaled as an element of natural food.

Second.—It is unsurpassed as a remedy in most and probably in all wasting diseases, where it relieves the stomach, rests over-taxed digestive organs, lubricates inflamed alimentary tracts and arrests their further congestion, satisfies most all demands of the system for a concentrated heat-producing food, and restores to a worn-out or broken-down tissue just such elements of repair as its reconstruction demands.
ter, 11th Verse, Genesis, proves the existence

Third.—It possesses a direct alterative effect in constitutional diseases. The 8th Chapof the olive tree in the earliest period of the world's history.

Fourth.—It exerts a distinctive influence upon the liver and apparently, also upon the kidneys. The benefits to be derived from olive oil in liver derangements are not at all chimerical.

Fifth.—Its reconstructive properties follow its external application quite as readily as when given internally, and in some cases the former seems to be preferred. The medical profession, then, has a deep interest in the culture of the olive tree, and the fostering to the utmost perfection of the industry of preparing a positively pure oil—such as may be placed in everybody's hands, without prejudice and without misrepresentation. Physicians have the same right to demand an absolutely unadulterated oil as they have to demand pure quinine, pure morphia, or any other drug, chemical or remedy. But the sick—they, who, suffering, need its balm, and would be the grateful recipients of its priceless virtues, have the strongest plea to enter at the bar of justice against its contamination and substitution. Dr. Graves fed fevers. I feel that had Graves lived in our days he would have fed fevers with olive oil. This was my experience in 1852, in my case of yellow fever, when I fed the fever with pure olive oil. The chief value of olive oil in fevers lies in its ability to be rapidly absorbed through the skin, and in this way to exert its peculiar properties. In all cases it will reduce the temperature of the body, which means a saving of tissue—a matter of vital importance. On account of its chemical constitution, it is especially adapted for the feeding of fevers, as before explained, and as it is so readily absorbed by the skin, leaving that substance in the best possible condition under the circumstances of its natural working, it stands unrivaled for this line of use. In measels and in scarlet fever, its use (by taking the warm oil and rubbing it in with the hand from the extremities inward) will so certainly cause the heat to drop, induce ease and quietness, perhaps sleep; obviate internal congestions, and generally tend to have the disease run a mild and uncomplicated course, that to the uninitiated the results will seem but little less than marvelous. Especially is this so if the body be first sponged with a hot alkaline wash. In malarial fevers a vegetable and fruit diet, in which the oil can be freely used, and the inunctions of the oil are followed in due time by relief, because of the relief that this treatment brings to the jaded liver. In typhoid fever the thorough rubbing in of as much oil as the skin will take, at periods properly preceding the diurnal rises of temperature, will do more good, is more grateful, less troublesome to apply, and rationally more scientific, than the treatment by cold water packs or immersion of the whole body in a bathtub filled with cold water. I am aware that the cold water treatment has apparently saved many lives and is based upon a plausible principle, but I am so thoroughly convinced that the oil treatment is more rational that I do not hesitate to draw a strong comparison.

In the disease of digestion and of the digestive tract the continued use of the oil has fully sustained all that I have heretofore had to say ot it, so that I need not again go over that ground. In the wasting diseases, of which consumption can be taken as the conspicuous type, the use of olive oil seems to be imperatively called for.

Because of its chemical composition it can do all that cod liver oil, even under the most favorable circumstances can be hoped to do. Besides, it possesses remedial properties that the animal oils do not posess, and it is so easily taken and assimilated, so much more palatable, and so free from nauseous after-effects, that we wonder that any one thinks of taking cod liver oil any more, when the superiority of olive oil can so readily be understood. But it has ever been hard for the human mind to break away from its medical fetiches, and of all lines of reformation the reformation of the theory and practice of medicine has been most hampered, delayed, harassed and opposed by superstition and its horde of uncanny allies. I am continuing to use and to advocate the use of olive oil in a class of nervous diseases characterized by great prostration of the powers and the progressive waste of nerve tissue. Here, again, as well as in the class of functional nervous diseases, are exhibited the needs of the system to be fed, rather than to be drugged, in all these cases the process of waste exceeding those of repair. The usual way of applying is by massage and inunctions once to thrice daily. With paralytics the operations of massage are most valuable. With epileptics, inunctions of oil immediately following a hot bath, and to be immediately followed by a sufficient rest in bed, induce the best results. From Dr. P. C. Remondio, of San Diego, I quote the following:

OLIVE OIL A REMEDY.

Olive oil has been used as a medicine in doses of from one to ten ounces. In administering oil, should the stomach reject it; sometimes, it occurs in taking olive oil in a large dose, or even a glass of milk, when they are strangers to the stomach, are very apt to produce the same effect.

Bearing this in mind, we should always, when giving oil in its large dose, use the precaution to add some wine, lime, or lemon juice, to insure its not offending the stomach.

In Intestinal Irritation. Children are often affected by a persistent harassing, dibilitating diarrhoea, due to the agglutination of some shred of tomato, grape or other fruit skin to the mucous lining of the intestines. The cause is here a simple mechanical irritation alone, to be removed by the use of olive oil.

As a Vermifuge (my belief). Olive oil is one of our safest vermifuges in the cases of children. It should be given in ounce doses, and frequently repeated. It is harmless, as it does not provoke active purging, and if the child's stomach does not reject it, it will do its work. In cases of tapeworm, it has often carried away the head, tail, and body, simply by its weight and volume.

In Bladder and Kidney Affections. In case of severe pains located in the region of the kidneys, olive oil taken internally, in medium doses, is beneficial in granting prompt relief. It has also been used with success in cases of painful urination, strangury, and in cases of what is popularly termed gravelly urine.

In Intestinal Affections. Simple diarrhoea, dysentery, colicky pains, flatulence or constipation, have all been relieved by the prompt and generous use of olive oil. Those diseases in children are peculiarly manageable with olive oil. There is nothing that will act more energetically in a case of imprisoned intestinal gases, accumulation of faces, or in cases of hernia or rupture, than a large dose of olive oil mixed with a few drops of turpentine; if the latter are not obtainable, then the oil should be given singly.

In General Diseases of Children. Teething children should always be oiled, the oil being applied at least twice daily. Nervous, fretful, peevish children obtain great relief by a warm water sponging and an oiling. Rickerty children, suffering from poor assimilation, will improve wonderfully on pure olive oil inunction. Children suffering with fever and a high degree of temperature can be relieved by a tepid sponge bath and an oiling. Cases of scarlet fever I always oil and keep on oiling from first to last; especially during convalescence is this oiling a great safeguard. Olive oil, taken both internally and by inunction, has often given results in cases of dropsy, either abdominal or general. In Europe it has been used with signal benefit in epidemics of yellow fever, and in Asia and Africa it has been used with equal benefit in the plague. In cases of neuralgia, rheumatism, gout, chronic skin diseases, in fact with diseases in general which are liable to result or originate in mal-assimilation, malnutrition, or imperfect blood depu-ration, olive oil has often afforded signal relief. In the fevers of adults it is equally of great value, being useful in reducing the temperature and nervous excitement.

Local Use. Olive oil, in connection with an equal part of lime water, makes excellent application to burned surfaces; relieves pain and promotes repair; have used it so mixed, in burns, scalds, powder wounds, and in skin abrasions. In powder accidents involving the eyes this makes a soothing and protective application. I have used the same mixture repeatedly in cases of smallpox, both in America and in West Indies. I used it with great benefit both in army and in civil practice. In conjunction with turpentine, it is an unequaled application to tense and tender abdomen that at times accompanies typhoid fever. As an antidote to poison olive oil has been given with success in cases of mushroom poisoning, being liberally mixed with powderer charcoal. "In general it may be said that olive oil is a safe and efficacious antidote in most cases of poisoning with the exception of phosphorous, where it should not be used."

From the many letters I have received where relief was obtained by the use of olive oil I will give a few statements:

A gentleman of San Francisco, whose wife had been a sufferer for seven years from gall stones, was completely cured by taking olive oil. She is today a well woman. She was under the care of a physician who said to her that his remedies were of no value and recommended that she try the use of olive oil.

Many have reported cures from piles, chronic constipation and indigestion. During the last month an important case of rheumatism was cured by the application of olive oil, reported from Ohio. Similar reports have been received from various places during the past years. Since the beginning of this year a most remarkable case was reported by a lady customer. The letter was as follows: "A woman living near me steeped a medicinal plant to give her little girl, of eight years. It was very bitter and the child begged not to take it, and promised to eat some of the seeds of the plant in place of drinking the tea. Her mother though no more of it until nearly three years later when the child began to act strangely and finally ended in St. Vitus Dance and almost complete idiocy. The mother learned from the other children that she had been in the habit of eating the weed whenever she went where it grew. I went in to see the child and took with me a bottle of olive oil. I poured it on the child's head until it ran down her face. The oil was positively green where it absorbed the poison through the pores of the skin and when the body was bathed with an abundance of oil the same results followed. The oil was a bright green. The oil was given internally two or three times a day in tablespoonful doses. The olive oil treatment was continued, both external and internal, with no other remedies. The child recovered both her physical and mental powers. The child is a young woman now, as this happened five years ago. There is no trace of any defect from the experience through which she passed. I have been using olive oil freely for the past eighty-five years and could tell of many other satisfactory results from its use."

A gentleman in Philadelphia, Pa., writes: "I have noticed a marked benefit in health since taking the olive oil regularly, a desert-spoonful three times daily."

A San Francisco gentleman wrote me in December as follows: "We (four of us) use about one quart bottle of olive oil a week. The children take it raw and really like it. I have colic sometimes; I do not know what to attribute it to. When the last attack was on I stopped the oil. The colic continued just the same. In desperation I resumed the oil and the colic stopped. It has not returned. As a further proof of the food value of olive oil I refer to a pamphlet of statements by Goddard E. D. Diamond, of San Francisco, now 105 years old, retaining all his faculties mental and physical, as a man of fifty, the use of olive oil has preserved this condition."

It is not my purpose to extend these reports from letters received; they are too numerous. I however desire to impress upon the public the importance of a liberal use of pure olive oil. All children are fond of it. Its use would save them from many pains and aches and from diseases common amongst them. How many women are constant sufferers from stomach troubles, and men especially confined to active business life are daily sufferers with pains in one form or another which could be obviated by taking the pure olive oil with their food. A competent cook can make judicious use of the oil in cooking potatoes, fish beans and other dishes which would add greatly to the flavor and taste.

The oil can be eaten on dry bread, on fresh and salted fish, on meats, on vegetables, and on salads. The last named when properly prepared is the greatest luxury. Half the quantity of food eaten would by the use of olive oil be of greater value to the system.

The one thing that the consumer must guard against is the spurious article. Adulteration and substitution are so universal that unless the greatest care is practiced deception in the quality will be forced upon consumers. Cotton seed oil is largely substituted for olive oil. All importations are adulterated with it, these mixtures are all more or less injurious, if the pure product of the olive oil cannot be obtained it is better not to use any oil as food or medicine. A part of cotton seed oil will not digest, it will not burn, it is a gum. To throw this indigestible potion out of the system is a great tax on the heart and digestive organs. If eaten in quantity it is sure to produce heart failure and all sorts of kidney troubles. Will the human family take this risk, merely because they can buy such poisonous stuffs at a few cents a bottle cheaper? Not only do they take the risk of the danger but they forego the great benefit to be derived by the use of pure olive oil. Detection is simple if the pure article can be had with samples to test the other oils.

No. 1. Put the pure article with samples to be tested in refrigerator where the thermometer will go as low as 35 Fah. and keep them in this temperature 48 hours. Most of the spurious samples will show plainly.

No. 2. Use the pure olive oil in oiling your floors. It will leave a beautiful polish and leave no grease to adhere to articles coming in contact with it. Use the adulterated product and if mixed with cotton seed a portion will evaporate. The other part will remain as a gum or pitch over which you cannot pass without its adhering to your shoes. You will be compelled, by either alcohol or spirits of turpentine, to cut it, that you can remove it from the floor.

No. 3. Pour on a hot stove plate, not hot enough to cause it to blaze, but to liberate the fumes. The cotton seed oil will emit a nasty odor, while the pure olive oil will give out the pleasant odor of the olive. For lubricating rapid moving machinery olive oil has no equal, while on the other hand cotton seed oil will so gum up the journals that it will be impossible to continue the motion. These tests will detect the adulteration in most of the so-called olive oils or salad oils, but for a complete analysis it is only a competent chemist who can give the proportions of the different substances that are contained in the mixtures.

Test No. 3 is important as it will detect cotton seed oil in other mixtures besides adulterated olive oil; for example, sardines, creamery butter, hogs' lard, cottolene, or any other mixture in which it is possible to add a part for the purpose of illegal gain or profit. Sardines formerly were immersed in olive oil and was a most delicious and healthy food. Of late years only cotton seed oil is used. All such should not be eaten. Cotton seed oil is especially prepared to give a yellow color to butter. Hog's lard, as put up in the slaughtering establishments, is about one-half cotton seed oil. Cottolene is principally cotton seed oil. The hot stove plate will detect the nasty odor in all these mixtures. Cotton seed oil has a value of about 3 1-2 to 4 cents a pound, while good, well-prepared leaf lard is worth from 6 to 10 cents a pound, pure creamery butter 25 to 40 cents and olive oil 60 cents, hence the temptation to adulterate by unscrupulous dealers.

Too much care cannot be exercised in the selection of our foods . We should demand of our grocer and druggist a guaranty as to the purity. They, on the other hand, can demand of the wholesale merchant or manufacturer a similar guaranty. We should not be called upon to rely upon the statements contained on the labels or the statements made by the dealers. No risks should be taken in which our health is involved. We should demand a guaranty. When we lend money we require a guarnty, taking every precaution to have proper security. Is our money more important than our health?

The oil that I use is guaranteed to be pure olive oil, is sweet to the taste, delicious to the palate, will not become rancid or musty.

Nature provides ample guides in selection of food, but the influence of custom, heredity and erroneous habits has preverted these natural guides, and have become, in mose cases, vitiated and consequently misleading. In selecting our food, science of comparative anatomy establishes the fact that man is naturally a grain, fruit and nut eating animal, therefore, if we desire to conform to nature we must observe this fact in the selection of food. But in mankind, a selection from grain, fruit and nuts, it is impirtant that these be thoroughly masticated, especially in the case of grain and nuts, which should be finely ground in order to yield their valuable store of nutritive elements. Mastication even with well pulverized food is important in order to thoroughly mix the saliva with the food and thus prepare it for the digestive process in the stomach, which consist of a thorough blending of it with the gastric juice. As each kind of food provides gastric juice adapted to its own digestion, the processes of digestion and also of elimination are greatly aided by the use of whole wheat instead of white flour so commonly used in bread making, and the very prevalent disease, constipation, is overcome. The risk of getting diseased meat is shown by the recent investigation into the beef supply of the army of the United States and the fact that the flesh even of healthy animals is productive of those disease caused by a superfluity uric acid, rheumatism, Bright's disease, headache and various nervous disorders should induce a fair trial of the vegetarian system.

To enjoy life is a subject which all should consider, but without a true system of self-government, in accordance with that which is beneficial to a true condition of living, we cannot expect freedom from disease and misery, and true happiness established. How often we hear such remarks repeated in churches as: "We have left undone those things we ought to have done, and have done those things we ought not to have done, and there is no health in us." And no wonder, when we consider the complete disregard in many, for that which tends to give true life, often abusing their constitution, by over-eating, drinking ,and other excesses, and obeying evil desires, in complete disregard to the Eternal Laws oı the Highest, which are written in the great book of nature.

What is needed in the present day, is men and women, of a determined nature, to do what is right and live noble, pure upright, chaste and honorable lives, seeking to preserve their bodies and souls as temples fit for man and woman to live in; by subduing all evil desires.

No matter what many clergy an dministers may say, the facts stand thus: The penalty for sin is, disease, misery, remorse of mind, which is a hell in the present life, and finally death; and the reward for good actions is, health and freedom from distress of mind and body, by overcoming evil with good. If all preachers and sayers were doers we might soon have the Kingdom established of Peace on Earth, and Good Will Amongst Men, and see the God of War and vain glory dethroned in the hearts of man, and right prevail with reason over brute force and tyranny. They may point to the grand buildings put up to worship in, as if it mattered greatly. Can any, wonder at the condition of the masses of people of the present day, when we consider the disregard of the true teaching of nature and of the Spirit of Peace, when also at the same time the majority of this world, often at the peril and loss of the lives of their fellowman; and at the same time ruining their health, and making false pleasures their misery and destruction.

THIRD EDITION.

Wisdom is a crown of life to those who find her, and in keeping health in body, mind and soul, rest and peace, with true and lasting happiness.—The Anatomy of Man, by Prof. Leo Weiner, of Harvard University.

When we eat meat we are eating the product of the earth at second-hand. The vegetation has been eaten by the animal and a large part of it converted into bone and tendon and wasted, and we eat only what is left and made into diseased flesh. Man has artificially become an omnivorous animal, in spite of the fact that anatomically he is a fruit-eating animal. It is an amusing and significant fact that the only typical omnivorous animal is the pig. Man is trying hard to be a pig. These classes are the carnivorous, or flesh-eating, the fruit-eating, the grass-eating and the omnivorous.

This question is one for our most serious consideration, for it is intimately connected, not only with our own physical welfare but with that of our children and posterity. We all know that the sins of the fathers are visited upon the children for several generations. Around us, on every hand we see melancholy illustrations of this terrible fact, in the hundreds of tuberculous and scrofulous children to be found in every large town, in those unfortunates who are crippled by gout and rheumatism, in the early graves which engulf so many consumptive young men and women, before they have reached the prime of life, and in the great multitudes of dyspeptics, suffering from deranged livers, and other invalids, whose number increases with the advance of medical science instead of decreasing. And it will while our children are taught, by early observation, that slaughter and cruelty are part of the established order of things as ordained by God, the relization of this ideal prospect is quite impossible, and therefore, those who support the custom of killing sentient creatures in order to devour their flesh, are upholding a system which bears the progress of mankind down. It also bears a close relation to the work of uplifting humanity. The success of such religious work depends largely upon the spiritual tone of professing Christians, and whilst all that is carnal in them is fostered and fed by the consumption of the flesh and blood of animals, those who labor to lead them to the higher states of spiritual experience will naturally be much hindered in their endeavor. Then, again, there is little hope of reforming a drunkard whilst he is feeding his cravings for stimulants by eating flesh, but if he abandons this habit there is hope. Nothing, probably, hinders the progress of the Gospel, in countries like India, more than the practice of Christians eating flesh.

The Brahminical law declared (1,000 years B. C.) that flesh eating was to be abandoned, because it involved slaughter and cruelty. The Buddhist is taught by his religion that it is contrary to the will of a benevolent God to kill animals wantonly, and much more so to eat them. How can he accept Christianity as a superior religion, when his hereditary instincts and religious belief lead him to consider that the flesh-eating missionary is on a lower plane of spirituality than himself. Should we listen to the teachings of cannibals if they came to instruct us? Yet converts are often known by the fact of their adopting this pernicious habit, and as the hindoos believe it to be a universal Christian practice, they reject the religion of Christ accordingly. I need not say any more to show that the question is at least one of grave consequence, as it must already be apparent to you. With the earliest impressions of childhood, we have received the idea that the most important article of our diet is animal flesh (or meat, as it is more politely called, in order to disguise somewhat its real nature), and that it is impossible to be vigorous without a liberal consumption of this type of food. In the case of the most of us this idea has been accepted without question or thought like many of our religious notions, and probably it has never been challenged. Occasionally, we have felt our spirits slightly depressed, when upon passing some slaughter house, perchance we have heard the dying groans of some wretched creature, and thus been reminded of the fact that the animals who provide our dinners have to suffer a violent death before we can eat them; but we have generally dismissed the melancholy reflection as hastily as possible with the thought that the cruel work has to be done, for humanity and for the animal kingdom, depend upon the response of the Christian world to this great question (which is every month destined to challenge attention more urgently). Let me assure you that nothing is further from my thoughts than any attempt to sit in judgment upon those who have never doubted the wisdom and lawfulness of eating animal flesh, because they have never been led to consider that any principle could be involved in the matter.

A very large number of reasons might be urged in support of the statement that the practice of eating the flesh of dead animals is morally wrong. The first two, if admitted to be valid, are alone sufficient to justify one in logically holding such a conviction, but I venture to believe that all of them are of such a nature as to commend themselves to your judgment, as being based upon sound reason and common sense. They are as follows, viz.:

1. That as man is stated by the leading scientist of the world to be a frugivorous (or fruit-eating) animal, not possessing either teeth suitable for tearing flesh or digestive organs by nature adapted to its assimilation (both of which are found in all the carnivorous), the voluntary consumption of the dead bodies of animals in a civilized country is a violation of one of the fundamental laws governing his being, and, therefore, totally unnecessary.

2. That the custom of eating flesh involves the infliction of an incalulable amount of suffering and torture upon countless thousands of sentient creatures, such enormities as are daily taking place, being utterly unjustifiable except upon the ground of absolute and unavoidable necessity.

As this necessity does not exist, the perpetration of those cruelties is morally wrong, being an outrage upon all human sentiment, and a violation of the Christian duty of showing mercy to the weak and defenseless. Those who purchase the flesh create the demand, and are aiders and abettors of the evil that is done to gratify their degenerate appetites—being accessories both before and after the fact.

3. That the consumption of animal flesh is the direct cause of an immense amount of human suffering and disease, which afflicts not only the consumers, but their children to the third and fourth generation.

4. That the barbarous practice is detrimental to man, it is to a large extent the cause of crime and vice, with which our and other lands are cursed, and no reform at present before the public would produce such permanent benefit to the community as the return to the natural food which was originally designed for man. In support, then, of my first statement, which is the most important of all, seeing that if it is established to your satisfaction, it ought not to be difficult to convince you, as earnest men and women, that the wholesale slaughter and abominable cruelties involved in flesh-eating are utterly unjustifiable. Let me call first, as witnesses, some of our leading scientists and medical men:

Linnaeus (whose zoological classification is generally accepted), places man with the anthropoid apes, at the head of the highest order of the mammiferous animals. The structure of those apes bears the closest resemblance to that of man, and they are all fruit-eaters in their natural state.

Prof. Sir Richard Owen, F. R. S., states: "That authropoids and all the quadrumana, derive their alimentation from fruits, grains, and other succulent vegetable substances, and the strict analogy which exists between the structure of those animals and that of man, clearly demonstrates his frugivorous nature."

Prof. Baron Cuvier says: "The natural food for man, judging from his structure, consists of fruit, roots and vegetables."

Prof. W. M. Lawrence, F. R. S., states: "The teeth of man, have not the slightest resemblance to those of carnivorous animals, and whether we consider the teeth, jaws, or digestive organs the human structure closely resmbles that of the frugivorous animals."

Prof. Ray tells us: "Certainly man was never made to be a carnivorous animal."

Prof. Sir Charles Bell, F. R. S., states: "It is, I think, not going too far to say that every fact connected with the human organization goes to prove that man was originally formed a frugivorous animal. This opinion is principally derived from the formation of his teeth and digestive organs, as well as from the character of his skin and general structure of his limbs."

Dr. Spencer Thompson writes: "No physiologist would dispute with those who maintain that man ought to live on vegetarian diet."

Dr. Alex Haig, F. R. C. P., in his famous work on "Uric Acid," writes: "That it is easily possible to sustain life on the products of the vegetable kingdom, needs no demonstration for physiologists, even if a majority of the human race were not constantly engaged in demonstrating it, and my researches show not only that it is possible, but that it is infinitely preferable in every way, and produces superior powers both of mind and body."

Dr. Oldfield, M. R. C. S., L. R. C. P., writes: "Today there is the scientific fact assured—that man belongs not to the flesh-eaters, but to the fruit-eaters. Today, there is the chemical fact that in the hands of all, which none can gainsay, that the products of the vegetable kingdom contains all that is necessary for the fullest sustenance of human life."

Sir B. W. Richardson, M. D., F. R. S., at a recent congress on Public Health, said: "He sincerely hoped that before the close of the century, not only would slaughter-houses be abolished, but that all use of animal flesh as food, would be absolutely abandoned."

A large number of such authorities could be quoted, but these being of such eminence, will suffice. Now for experimental evidence:

A report upon the food of the agricultural laborers of Europe taken by order of the English Government and cited in the "Anthropological Review," of 1872, tells us that in Sweden, Russia, Italy, Bavaria, Ireland and Holland most of the peasants do not eat flesh, whilst in Scotland, Switzerland and Prussia the laborers only take it on rare occasions. The same is true of many of the Norwegians and Finns. The majority of the enterprising Japanese, the Brahmins, Hindoos, and devout Buddhists of India, the porters and soldiers of Turkey (not the Kurds), the Egyptian soldiery, and the renowned Sikhs and Ghoorkas live without eating flesh, as do the Benedictine, Franciscan, Dominican and Trappist monks. The conquering soldiers of Rome and Sparta, the athletes and wrestlers of Greece were generally abstainers from flesh meat, and thousands of vegetarians, of long experience, in our own country, today, can testify, that they are happier, healthier, and more vigorous than when they ate it. Those various types of mankind number, collectively, hundreds of millions and inhabit every variety of climate.

COMMON SENSE OBSERVATIONS.

I.

That Plantain Leaf is an antidote for the bite of the tarantula. I saw the tarantula bite the toad, the toad leap and nip the plantain leaf and fight back repeatedly. I removed the plantain leaf, and after the next tarantula bite the toad swelled, discolored and died. It was hard on the toad, but a lesson to me.

II.

That the Exhausted Horse, if turned out to select food for himself, will find the kind of herb which will produce the correct remedy for whatever derangement of the internal organs may be his trouble. It is so with the other members of the animal kingdom, except man, who if left to himself is almost sure to eat the wrong thing because it suits his taste, or his degenerate appetite.

III.

That Strong Black Coffee is a better remedy for relief from ague than quinine. This I discovered while providing supplies for men in my employ in a malarial region. There was no cream, and the black coffee was used as a tonic, but to my surprise, it cut the ague off smack—smooth. Black, strong, and enough of it is effective as a remedy for ague.

IV.

That the Skunk is a good chemist, and if he can get access to nature's laboratory he knows how to compound ingredients and impound them in his body as weapons of defense against all comers. If caged and detained, his ammunition is gone, and to surrender is his portion.

V.

That Yellow Jaundice can be drawn out of the body by the proper application of the red onion. Use red onion, because of its quadruple strength, by splitting it into halves. Apply the flat side of the onion next to the body, under the arms, back of the knees, in the groins, and at the bottom of the feet, renewing frequently, and the juandice will take to the onion as electricity to the wire.

VI.

That Asphixiation is relieved by the immediate use of the strongest emetic at command.

Twice in my life have I been asphxiated and upon both occasions has relief come quick and permanent by an emetic. "In the time of peace prepare for war" is a good practice in this decade of poor gas.

VII.

That Diphtheria, or any form of sore throat, may realize immediate relief by using a gargle of sulphur. One teaspoonful of powdered sulphur in a glass two-thirds full of warm water, stirred with the finger (which is better than a spoon), until well dissolved, and used as a gargle once an hour (oftener in a critical case) will effect a speedy cure. If patient is too weak to gargle, blow the dry sulphur into the throat through quill or paper funnel, which will destroy the fungus.

VIII.

That the Best Remedy For A Cold is a red onion stew. When I say red onion, I mean red, for the reason of its strength. Use the white onion only as a necessity. Make a stew of red onions, and plenty of it; quarantine yourself, and eat all you can, drinking the juice, and you will not have long to wait for relief. But you will be told by others that there is a decided onion atmosphere in the community.

X.

That Two Pebbles kept in the mouth and

rolled about by the tongue, will so excite the glands as to produce sufficient saliva to satisfy thirst for a considerable period of time, and prevent the desire for cold water in large draughts, which is at all times a source of possible injury.

XI.

That Sun Tan can be removed in the short space of forty-eight hours by taking sour buttermilk and mix with it wheat bran, until the solution becomes like a poultice. Lay it over the face for two nights, and on the third day the skin will appear soft, smooth and white as virgin beauty.

XII.

That To Preserve The Beauty Of Youth into a good old age, one need only to observe the laws of hygiene. If you would have a fair complexion leave off the use of coffee, tea and slaughtered meats, and make free use of olive oil and fruits in season, of which nothing compares with the apple. To this, rise with the sun, improve every hour, keep good natured and in harmony, and retire with the children.

XIV.

That Olive Oil, for culinary purposes, excels all other oils, including butter. Try it when you fry eggs; try it in the preparation of fried potatoes; try it in the frying of fish, especially fresh mountain trout; try it when you want a delicate dish of fried oysters, and try it for any and all purposes in which you ordinarily use lard, or butter, but do not use cheap, adulterated cotton seed oil as a substitute for the pure article, for a part of it is a gum that will neither digest, nor will it burn, it will cause heart failure.

MISERY TURNED TO COMFORT.

A few of the many diseases cured by the use of pure, fine olive oil that I use for myself. The only requirement is the knowledge of how to use the olive oil, to cure those ailments: Gall Stones, Appendicitis, Deafness, Tapeworm, Indigestion, Gravely Urine, Bright's Disease, Stiff Joints, Ossification, Fevers, Scrofula, Eruptions, Chronic Gout, Skin Disease, Catarrh of the Stomach, Liver and Kidney Trouble, Measels, Stomach Trouble, Constipation, Yellow Jaundice and Dropsy, Bronchial Trouble, Yellow Fever, Weak or Sore Eyes, Rheumatism, Lumbago, Smallpox, Eczema, and for every kind of fever. Gravel, Kidneys, Urinary Acid, Salt Rheum, Spring Fevers.

My New Book, Secret of Long Life, in fourth edition, is in many ways more plain than the present one.

Price for single copy, Fifty Cents. And I will send them to your postoffice address post paid on receipt of postoffice order for Fifty Cents.

G. E. D. DIAMOND,
Oakland, Cal.

The fine, pure olive oil will prevent ossification, which brings about obstructions in the blood. Arterial ossification is caused by calcareous deposits, and to prevent such deposits in the system take two tablespoonfuls of olive oil stirred into a saucer full of apple sauce night and morning. It is a sure cure for indigestion and for stomach, liver and kidney trouble.

THE PURE, FINE OLIVE OIL.

How to remove gall stones with it: Take a tablespoonful of olive oil three or four times a day for (2) days, then take a half pint of olive oil on going to bed and lay on the right side. Save the stool, wash it out and you will find the gall stones in the bottom of the chamber.

THE PURE, FINE OLIVE OIL.

Removes tapeworm: Take a pint of olive oil and it will carry it away out of the stomach. Don't eat for six hours.

Meat for food I consider unfit to eat. It causes scrofula, cancer, ulcer, tumors, boils, eruptions, indigestion, rheumatism, liver and kidney trouble, Bright's disease. It causes stomach trouble. It causes headache and fever. It is bad for rheumatism and constipation. When we eat meat we are eating the product of the earth second-hand. The vegetable has been eaten by the animal and a large part of it converted into bone and tendon and wasted, and we eat what is left and made into diseased flesh. You can obtain from any reputable physician who will tell you that meat-eating is heating to the blood; that it is especially a stimulant rather than food, and that there is great danger of the transmission of various serious diseases from animal to man.

NATURE'S FOOD FOR MAN.

By nature man is a fruit-eating animal. The three main divisions of food are: the carbonaceous, which supplies the bodily heat; the nitrogenous, which builds the tissues of the body; and the phosphatic, which forms the blood-salts and furnishes food required by the brain. The amount varies greatly; use varies according to climate. Low temperature, increase of carbonate; corresponding decrease in high temperatures. Carbonaceous foods, starch, sugar, fats, etc., supply heat and vital power. Starch is found in all cereals—wheat barley, corn peas, beans, rice, buckwheat, tapioca, arrowroot, potatoes, parsnips, carrots. Grape sugar is the natural body fuel. "I Prefer Olive Oil" for body fuel. It is not bilous. A certain amount of fat is essential to adults, especially nervous people. The fat of the body is the surplus of starch and sugar which has been stored beyond the bodily needs. It repairs tissue and supports muscular activity.

MISERY TURNED TO COMFORT.

A few of the many diseases cured by the use of pure, fine olive oil.

The only requirement is the knowledge of how to use the olive oil. To cure these ailments, gall stones, appendicitis, deafness, tape worm, indigestion, gravely urine, Bright's disease, stiff joints, ossification, fevers, scrofula eruptions, chronic gout, skin disease, catarrh, liver and kidney trouble, measles, stomach trouble, constipation, yellow jaundice and dropsy, bronchial trouble, yellow fever, weak or sore eyes, rheumatism, lumbago, smallpox, eczema, and for every kind of fever, gravel in the kidneys, urinary acid, salt rheum, spring fevers.

My new book—Secret of Long Life.

Price, single copies fifty cents. I will send them to you post paid, on receipt of post-office order for fifty cents.

G. E. D. DIAMOND,

Oakland, Cal.

FOURTH EDITION.

THE SECRET OF LONG LIFE.

A Son Worshiper, or the greater power, if there be one beyond; "Why Are We?" The year is passing—its day will soon be ended and gone from us forever. As we watch its silent progress into the realm of fading memories, we may well pause in the hurry and rush of life and ask ourselves the pertinent question—where are we? The people are not food reformers as they used to be. The cleric is more guilty in this respect than the layman. "The future," it has been said, "is with the vegetarians." We interpret this as meaning "the near future." Vegetarianism is in the air. We might naturally expect the Church to be the pioneer and leader of the well-being of the people—well-being, physical, moral and social. The fact must be deplored that the Church is not to the front in this, or any movement of reform, Vegetarianism she regards in the light of "heresy;" with it she has no sympathy, and upon its disciples she has no blessing to bestow. Yet it is a curious but interesting fact that this movement owes much to the life and work of the clergyman that had to go outside of the church to do his work. A reformer parson does not find, in the church by laws established, a bed of roses. She has to be a willing slave to King Custom; she has accepted and proclaimed the Gospel, "whatever is, is right!" She is tory to the backbone. Reform means, or should mean, the natural development of the principles of Christianity,—and the resolute assertion of those principles in our ordinary, everyday social life. Our social state is none too clean. I consider her duty it is to be its sponsor. Why should not the Church be able to persuade man of the truth; by, which we will be able to choose the good and avoid the evil? A new order of clergy is springing up—but to bring in the Social Reformation they will have to be abstaineis from flesh meat. It is this fact that the vegetarianism is so radical, going to the heart and root of things—which make it unpopular in the past, too many reforms which touch the pocket that are wrapped up in food reform. It brings us face to face with land monopoly; it confronts us with vested interests of many kinds, with a whole army of brewers, distillers, graziers, butchers, slaughtermen and others; our unpopularity, if unpopular we be, should not cause us regret; it is a good sign, the best of signs; it assures us that we are on the side of Truth, that we are treading in the footprints of the Son of Man, that we are asserting, as He would have us assert, the priciples of Justice. Reforms have never been popular. The emancipation of slaves was carried in the teeth of a most deadly opposition; the emancipation of those other slaves—our women—has not been a wholly popular movement. Reformers will not, however, rest content until women have been granted equal rights with men. Are men able by the force of pressing age—long experience—to grasp a future life for themselves, and deny it to women? Are they able at length to include women in the circle of God's love, and exclude all others of His creatures? The same law of physical life holds good for all animals. Who shall say that the natural laws by which God has developed mind and soul consciousness in man are not equally applicable in the evolution of all life? Why should it not do the same in the case of animals, who suffer just as unequally, just as inexplicably, just as terribly, as man suffers? The same things occur in animal life as in human life. The great St. Bernard braves the bitter frost to save a wayfaring stranger, the brave Newfoundland leaps into the stormy waves to save the drowning child, and sinks exhausted. The argument is the same; the premises are the same; the conclusion is the same. "Made perfect by suffering" is as much applicable to the earlier stage of life as to the latter; as fittingly appropriate to the suffering animal in non-human shape who has much humanity, as to the suffering animal in human shape who has little humanity hereafter. Of all the tender love of a mother, the anguish of child-birth, the cares and solicitude, the toil, the labors, and self-stinting to give the best of her life to her offspring, sufferings of motherhood to a common life in the Hereafter. We shall be able to understand something more of the universal Love not restricted to a few creatures called man, but widely extended to all His creation. Many a nation—aye, one as highly developed as the Jewish in the time of the Maccabees—has denied that women are not fit to enter the heaven of the blessed, and if they have a future at all, it must be in Gehanna of Destruction. It does not matter that human life is degraded and sentient life cruelly tortured, to any of these worthy people! It really would never do—the proprieties of society must be maintained at any cost, and it would never do to turn against "meat," because that would upset all the shooting parties and the hunting, and then the wealthy folk would have nothing to do!—a very sad state of affairs. Ye Gods! Fancy wasting the wealth of the nation in this way. Our preacher, he has found chapter and verse to support all his cannibalistic tendencies, blissfully forgetting that "every living thing" can be quoted to support the eating of missionaries. Of course, it is not his work to preach those things which develop the Christ spirit of universal kindness—he must only preach truths and platitudes which act as spiritual narcotics upon his hearers. It would be most unwise to start and preach the Food Reform gospel of kindness from the pulpit—pew rents have to be thought of! On conversation with a reverend brother I must recount. When asking what business could be recommended for his son, a fine, vigorous lad of thirteen years of age, I suggested to him to let the lad learn the butchering business, being a trade of great refinement! With a look of the most utter amazement, he asked what I meant by such a suggestion, and when I told him that it was a legalized trade, constant, and well paid, he blazed up in righteous indignation. "Why, in six months my boy would be a wreck, for such a disgusting business would ruin all his finer sensibilities, and, besides unfitting him for any refined society, it would make him into a brute." I gasped! Great heavens, this from a flesh-eater, too! Then came my turn, and I asked him how he, a minister of the Christ-spirit, dared to support, in the slightest degree, a trade which he himself recognized would wreck and ruin his son. Poor Rev., you don't mind making somebody else's boy learn the trade! Somebody else's son does not matter at all—and if other little lads have to learn the brutal business, of course you can preach to them nicely on Sunday and tell them to be kind to animals! It sounds so nice! Some time or other the Church will come into line—just as it has had to do with all other great reforms, but it is a sad state of things that where the welfare of the race is affected, the Church has to be led by "outsiders," instead of leading the way herself. I feel very much interested in the Christian institution, and I have said that the greatness of any individual is measured by the extent of her influence over her contemporaries for that which is good and true, and the permanence of the principles which she represents, that individual whose influence reaches the furthest in the greatest age of the world's history. This is undoubtedly the age of greatest achievement, the greatest in illumination, in the understanding and application of principles, of attainment in high and noble enterprises, with Longer Life and more pleasure in living it.

Nature's Law by Advanced Thinkers in every nation are now giving earnest attention to the subject of the prolongation of human life to a period extending a long way beyond the century, and there is every prospect that an important amount of light will be thrown upon the subject before long, for research is being earnestly made upon the "new thought." If it should be discovered, as seems to be highly probable, that the mind and character are essential conditions to the great secret which has baffled the world's ages, what an impetus will be given to the study of religion, what a premium will be placed upon goodness of the real type. Without doubt, many men who would not deny themselves a single sinful gratification or make any effort to live the Christlike life, in the hope of gaining blessedness in some future state, would consider no sacrifice too great in order to secure the secret of a prolonged existence in the physical body. I am hopeful I have been making investigations concerning the relationship of daily habit to longevity. I sent a series of questions to a number of centenarians who are living, and, judging from their replies, I have come to the conclusion that the fact of a man being tall or short, stout or lean, has little to do on his chance of reaching a hundred years, and that the most important point is food, drink, and the care of the body. The majority of these centenarians reported that they were either small meat-eaters or ate no meat at all, and that the staple food of nearly all was vegetable and fruit. Most of them abstained from spirituous liquors, but not from the simple wine of the country.

Most of them claimed the possession of cheerfulness of temper and alluded to the avoidance of excitement and worry about daily trifles. Sanguineness and content tend to bring about length of days is my opinion, and a certain degree of stoicism is also worth cultivating. Those who lead a feverish, hurry-scurry life are not likely to live a hundred years. More than forty years ago I commenced to warn the public to beware of tuberculous milk and meat, and today every state is ringing with warnings against this danger uttered by the highest medical and municipal authorities. Just in the same manner as society is slowly waking up to the fact that the eating of consumptive cattle and the drinking of their unboiled milk is dangerous, so will it, before many years have elapsed, realize the great truth that wanton and needless butchery for the supply of unnatural and injurious food is a violation of moral as well as physical law.

How few of us realize the great mystery of Life as manifest in this world of ours. How few of us ever stop to think about the countless millions of human beings who have lived, struggled and died in bygone ages, long before historic times. In many parts of the world traces of civilization which existed thousands of years ago have been discovered, but attention has recently been directed afresh to the subject by the account of researches made in the earth-mounds in the United States. These prove conclusively the fact that in the dim past, probably thousands of years before Egyptian dynasties were heard of, races of men existed in America who were first-rate mechanics—as evidenced by the weapons they made, and good surveyors—as the exact proportions of their enclosures, temples and mausoleums declare. They dwelt in villages and towns, they were fond of their children and made them little toys, such as miniature axes, etc.; they made costly ornaments as well as weapons of war; they were skilled in pottery and they worshipped the Deity through his greatest symbol, the sun, as their sculptures reveal. They practiced cremation in addition to other forms of burial; they held the ties of family to be sacred—for fathers have been found buried with their children—and they believed in immortality, for in many instances their best treasures have been found interred with them, as if they expected to be able to use them in another life. And yet this unknown race lived so long ago that no trace of human hair has been found with their skeletons—as is often the case in Egyptian tombs—although their mound—like mausoleums which are often covered with virgin forest and trees of long centuries' growth, have been built of calcined earth, which has kept the remains perfectly array. In most cases their bones have dropped to powder soon after discovered, and, brought to the air, they turn to dust.

To enjoy life is a subject which all should consider, but without a true system of self-government, in accordance with that which is beneficial to a true condition of living, we can not expect freedom from disease, and misery, and true happiness established! When we consider the complete disregard in many, for that which tends to give true life, often abusing their constitution by over-eating, improper food, drinking, and other excesses, and obeying evil de sires, in complete disregard of the penalty of which are written in the great book of nature and many of which are contained in the Natural Law; in the keeping of which is life and the gaining of self-control, with freedom from disease. Many, seem to think that because the father lived in many cases, as do many of the present generation, on a level lower than that of animals, we should do likewise; but a great portion of the rising generation seek to live in the true standard External Life, without death to body, which is spoken of by John viii, 51, and xl, 26.

What is needed in the present day is men and women of a determined nature to do what is right and live noble, pure, upright, chaste, and honorable lives, seeking to preserve their bodies as temples fit for men and women to live in by, subduing all evil desires. No matter what many clergy and ministers may say, the facts stand thus: The penalty for sin is disease, misery., remorse of mind, which is a hell in the present life, and finally death; and the reward for good morals is Health, Life, and Peace to body and mind, a state of Paradise, and freedom from distress of mind and body, by overcoming evil with good. Who can be happy, whilst following desires and wishes instilled into our minds by, evil, causing loss of energy and waste of our substance from the system, which, if retained, would build and replenish with good material. A fool can soon ruin a constitution which may take a wise man years to build up. The ideal set up for us to imitate is indulged in by many,, but how many seek to live up to it? For actions prove, not professions alone; preaching is one thing but practice another; if all preachers and sayers were doers, we might soon have the kingdom established of Peace on Earth, and good will amongst men, and see the God of war, and vain glory dethroned in the hearts of man; and right prevail with reason over brute force and tyranny. Who will sacrifice honor, sympathy, charity, kindness, self-esteem and honesty of purpose, to be highly approved of by man, and for sake of gold.

Can any wonder at the condition of the mass of the present day, when we consider the disregard of true teaching of good will, and of the Spirit of Peace; when also at the same time the majority of the people are seeking for personal advancement in the sight of the world, often at the peril and loss of the lives of their fellowman; and to their hurt; whilst boasting of their great charity and love of their fellow-countrymen, yet often squandering as much in one night's debauchery as would keep some families for weeks in plenty; and at the same time ruining their health, and making false pleasures to their destruction.

Wisdom is a crown of life to those who find Her, and in keeping health is lasting happiness, and in living a proper life is found all.

CAN WE LIVE A THOUSAND YEARS?

Why not? We are beginning to see that old age, with its accompanying ailments, might for a long time—how long we can not now say—be avoided by wise living. Barring accident, poverty (which always means slow starvation in some form), and such conditions are due solely, to human folly, I do not see why any one need be ill. I will go further, and say that I do not see any inherent necessity for such a state of health to cease, if man could abolish poverty and accidents and would resolve to be wise, not to-morrow, but to-day. I can not see where and why Providence could, or would, arrest an existence wisely planned and wisely lived from the beginning—would say to the wise liver: "Thus far shalt thou go and no farther." In other words, I consider it a conservative prophecy, that many such wise ones may live to, and even exceed, the age attained by Methuselah. When you are in perfect health, as I claim to be, you will feel that there is much truth in the saying: "Time was made for slaves."

My prophecy, however, can be verified or disproved only as successive years unfold themselves. I await this future and its revelations with an unfaltering trust in my dietetic teachings—a trust grounded on eighty-five years' successful application of these teachings. And I have revised my book, The Secret of Long Life, on those lines of my one hundred and ten years **young**, the first day of last May nineteen hundred and six, now writing my fourth edition to my book, for next July; after more than one hundred and ten years of active life, in possession and perfect use of every sense and faculty unimpaired.

Puffs under the eyes, red nose, pimpled, blotched, greasy face, don't always mean hard drinking as much as it shows that there is Bile in the Blood. It is true drinking and overeating overloads the stomach, but failure to assist nature in regularly disposing of the partially digested lumps of food that are taken into the stomach and allowed to rot there, is what causes all the trouble. Flush the sewer with a small bowl of apple sauce with two tablespoons full of pure olive oil, two tablespoons full of molasses, one teaspoon full of soda stirred well, mix, then take a cup of hot water before and after eating the apple sauce; it will flush the sewer sweet and clean. And it will help nature, and help you, and keep the system from filling up with poisons, and clean out sores that tell of the system's rottenness bloated by bile, the figure becomes unshapely, the breath foul, the eyes and skin yellow; in fact, the whole body kind of fills up with filth. Every time you neglect to help nature you lay the foundation for just such troubles. This prescription will carry poison out of the system without gripe or pain. Keep it up for two or three weeks, and it will help the liver and kidneys, clean up the bowels, and you will feel like a new man. Your blood will become rich, face look clean, eyes bright. Get one of Captain Diamond's books, Secret of Long Life, or How to Live in Three Centuries, and take as directed. And if you are not satisfied, you get your money back. It is worth many a dollar to you. It has recipes for curing Gall Stones, Tape Worm, Eczema, Fever, Appendicitis, Bronchial Trouble, Constipation, Stomach Trouble, Kidney and Liver Trouble. It cures Flux or Diarrhoea and Bloody Piles. It is a Positive Cure for those complaints. It never fails to cure Piles, etc. Clean up once a week, sure.

THE SECRET OF LONG LIFE.

A book which bears the above title, the third edition, written by the author after I had past my one hundred and fifth year of age, which has already reached its third edition, although consisting of some 100 and more pages, contains so much valuable information for the Food Reform that you would like to know something about its contents. Eighty-five years ago I commenced to make clinical research concerning the cause of headaches, from which I suffered severely, and having discovered that an excess of uric acid in the blood produced the same, I was led to investigate the action of this poisonous substance on the constitution. For years researches were continued day by day with a patience, and in this valuable treatise which has already become a text-book in the medical world, the results of those investigations are set forth. The conclusions, that meat, eggs, and tea, having proved that an excess of uric acid accompanied headache and mental depression, and I found that animal food contained a large amount of this substance. I abstained from meat altogether and found the headaches to cease and the uric acid in the blood to be diminished. In consequence of this I have now been an abstainer from flesh of all kinds for the past eighty years. When the blood is alkaline it can retain in solution a larger amount of uric acid and the elimination of this noxious poison is thus made possible by means of the liver and the kidneys. If the acidity of the blood is increased by acid food or drinks, uric acid at once becomes precipitated in the capillaries, joints and tissues, causing headache, gout, and other troubles. By carefully continuing a diet which is free from uric acid, I was able to reduce my headaches from one a week down to one in eighteen months, and found it wise to avoid tea and coffee as well as animal food, for the simple reason that the tea and caffeine, although not uric acid itself, yet has somewhat similar effects upon the constitution. The fact that a liberal consumption of tea produces a rapid increase in the amount of uric acid in the system, and I commend this fact to the consideration of those who, whilst endeavoring to follow a hygienic diet, sometimes suffer from dyspepsia and similar ailments, probably owing to tea and coffee.

After these long years of experimentation, the verdict concerning animal food is as follows: "My experience leads me to answer the question of the quantity of animal food necessary for nutrition, as follows: no animal food at all is necessary, for the whole of the required nitrogen can be got from the vegetable kingdom, but as milk and cheese appear to have no power of increasing the excretion of uric acid, they may be used along with the vegetable foods. The analytical tables published in this book show that beef tea contains seven grains of uric acid per pound, meat juice forty-nine grains per pound, and meat extract sixty-three. The consumption of eggs invariably bring about a rise in the excretion of uric acid and all the evil effects of its passage through the blood, thus pointing to the fact that they should be consumed only at occasional intervals.

Amongst the numerous diseases which attribute to the accumulation of uric acid in the blood or its deposit in the system, are rheumatism, gout, diabetes, and Bright's disease.

The health of the English army in India and the native army, by Surgeon Colonel P. de H. Haig, who states that the native army lives chiefly on grain and rice. The English soldier in India eats seven times as much meat as the native soldier, and the result is that the following diseases exist in the below mentioned ratio:

	English.		Native.
Alcoholism	54	to	1
Rheumatic Fever	5	to	1
Gout	3	to	1
Colic	12	to	1
Bright's Disease	3	to	1
Disease of the Liver	12	to	1
Dyspepsia	4	to	1
Piles	4	to	1
Suicide	6	to	1

The following sentences, coming as they do from the medical world:

Here again in England, do we not die younger and in greater numbers than there is any necessity for? In America, the question is, are we not afflicted with an infinite number of diseases which cause far more pain and misery than is at all necessary? Are we not given to all kinds of debauchery and excess, and have we not huge asylums full of lunatics and prisons full of criminals? Let me here impress upon your mind the secret of long life: it is our natural food, vegetables, fruit, nuts, and cereals. I do look upon all these things as serious and widespread diseases in the human race, and as I am not one of those who believe that Nature herself, if she had a free hand, would tend to destroy us, but ratner to preserve what is good, and eliminate what is evil; and further, I cannot believe that the tendency to these evils is part of the ground plan of Nature's work, or that the unalterable bias to have headache, epilepsy, mental depression, mania, and their results—murder or suicide—alcoholism, cocainism, etc., is originally planted in our nerve centers, I am driven to the conclusion that not a few of those evils are the result of unnatural conditions, and that prominent among those is unnatural diet, the evil action of which we are now in a position to follow out more completely through the knowledge of the powerful effects of urates on the function and nutrition of the whole body.

Such a provisional conclusion is justified by my own experience and results. I was originally told that my tendency to headache, high arterial tension, and other evils, was inherited—in fact, a part of my structure and function, though it might be modified and relieved by drugs, could not be eradicated, and no one ever suggested a radical change of diet. By great good fortune, and more or less by chance, I found out that a change of diet was the one thing needful, and what is practically a complete cure has resulted. I have now only one subject for regret, namely, that I did not find this out earlier in life, as I cannot undo the evils and injuries that were accomplished while the warnings of functional disturbance remained unheeded through ignorance of their causation.

To a very large extent, therefore, I disbelieve in inherited weakness, innate delicacy, in so far as such expressions apply to the diseases mentioned. I believe that much the same argument applies to nearly every disease mentioned in this book, and that while certain anatomical or physiological peculiarities may undoubtedly dispose certain individuals to suffer sooner than others, or in one way rather than in another, nevertheless the food factor is common to all of them, and its adequate consideration and treatment will always result in prevention or cure. The first step towards this object is the full and complete recognition of the fact that for practical purposes they are diet diseases, and that gout and rheumatism, for instance, may depend quite as much on the inheritance of the dollars necessary to obtain meat and wine as of any anatomical or physiological peculiarities.

THE AUTHOR.

Christmas festival no mere selfish time of enjoyment than one fraught with benefit to ourselves and others. Let each take home the question and answer it according to conscience: Shall Christmas mean to us self-indulgence or self-sacrifice? Adherence to humane principle or allegiance to barbaric fashion and custom?

Our Christian civilization is but a thin veneer overlaying inherent barbarism. The stony-heartedness of modern society at the present day.

Christmas—the Festival of Slaughter—"A very unpleasant way of putting it!" exclaims some easy-going upholder of our national customs, who loves a flesh dinner at any price; "but how true," reply those who rather than mingle their thanksgiving and rejoicing with the suffering and sacrifice of the dumb creation, have dared to look below the surface and resolved to make their actions, as far as they can, consistent with the message of "Peace and good will." True, it is not a pleasant picture, but yet it is well that each mind should lift the veil for a moment and let itself realize what the preparation for this annual festivity involves to the innocent animal world. But how many realize what germs of death and disease lie hidden in the tissues of those bodies, so soon to become food for the human subject? Truly there is a Nemesis for every broken law, and herein we trace the mute avenging of the animals' woes. The slaughter of a fine Chrictmas dinner appeared on the cover of a religious journal, the editor of which preaches and evangelizes according to his light, but I have no hesitation in pronouncing it to be an outrage, not only upon Christian and human sentiment, but even upon good taste and decency. And when the people flock in crowds and pay their money to witness butchering competition, when the whole country is eager to obtain reports of prize fights which are taking place, when women by tens of thousands are deaf to every protest that appears in the secular press concerning the decorating of their heads with the bodies of parent birds who are slaughtered in vast numbers to their vanity, Christian nations, by its legislators, license men to torment defenseless animals to their heart's content the whole year round. Or, perchance, they will be boiled down and thy condensed remains will find sepulchre in the stomach of some pious but deluded soul, who thinks he believes in the obligation to be just and merciful. Some good folks will doubtless find interest and even merriment in gazing upon thee, and think of what thy poor suffering body will become when transformed into a noxious fluid for their delectation. Some of them even recognize thee not only as a fellow creature, but as a brother, and yet can regard, without the slightest qualm of conscience, the thought of thy murder and consumption. Nevertheless, the pious claim there is a Judge of all the earth who will do Right, and who will, moreover, right thy wrongs eventually, and recompense in some other state of existence for the injustice and cruelty which thou and those who like thee are immolated upon the altar of man's tyranny, are called upon to endure. A Heaven-sent prophet once declared that the time would come at last when "he that slayeth an ox shall be regarded as he that slayeth a man"; when that day arrives, thy flayed limbs will no longer decorate the streets of Christian cities, to whet the palates of such as lay great stress on the singing of psalms and the making of long prayers, the generation of man who then inhabit the earth will blush with shame for the degradation and barbarity of their forefathers, and the groaning of creation will have to some extent ceased! This is later than when our forefathers were cannibals, Eating Human Flesh.

FLESH-EATING.

The question is one for our most serious consideration; it is intimately connected with our own physical welfare, of our children and posterity. We all know that the sins of the fathers are visited upon the children for several generations. Around us on every hand we see melancholy illustrations of this terrible fact, in the hundreds of tuberculous and scrofulous children to be found in every large town and city, in the early graves which engulf so many consumptive young men and women before they have reached the prime of life, and in the great multitudes of dyspeptics, sufferers from deranged livers. A change is needed, when cruelty and suffering shall be done away with forever. And man shall live out his full length of days. But whilst our children are taught by early observation that slaughter and cruelty are part of the established order of things as ordained by God, the realization of this ideal prospect is quite impossible. Those who support the custom of killing sentient creatures, in order to devour their flesh, are upholding a system which bars the progress of mankind from a higher and better state. It also bears down the work of uplifting humanity, in them is fostered and fed the consumption of the flesh and blood of animals. Then again, there is little hope of reforming a drunkard whilst he is feeding his craving for stimulants by eating flesh, but if he abandons this habit, there is. Nothing, probably, hinders the progress of the missionary in countries like India more than the practice of eating flesh. The Brahminical law declared (1000 years B. C.) that flesh eating was to be abandoned, because it involved slaughter and cruelty.

The Buddhist is taught by his religion that it is contrary to the will of a benevolent God to kill animals wantonly, and much more so to eat them. How can he accept Christianity as a superior religion, when his hereditary instincts and religious belief leads him to consider that the flesh-eating missionary is on a lower plane of spirituality than himself? Should we listen to the teachings of cannibals if they came to instruct us? Hindoos believe it to be a wicked practice; they reject the religion of Christ accordingly. I need not say any more to show that the question is at least one of grave consequence.

With the earliest impressions of childhood, we have received the idea that the most important article of our diet is animal flesh, and that it is impossible to be vigorous and strong without it. In the case of the most of us this idea has been accepted without thought (like many of our religious notions), when upon passing some slaughter house, perchance we have heard the dying groans of some wretched creature, and have thus been reminded of the fact that the animals who provide our dinners have to suffer a violent death before we can eat them. It is rather startling to be roused by the suggestion that the practice which is the result of it is morally wrong. But this also deals with our responsibility as aiders and abettors of the vast amount of cruelty inseparable from this custom, men and women, to endeavor to find out whether it is defensible or not from a moral standpoint; which, in my opinion, should lead you to decide the issues, what blessed prospects for our animal kingdom, depend upon the response of the Christian world to this great question which is ever destined to challenge attention more urgently.

Let me assure you that nothing is farther from my thoughts than any attempt to sit in judgment upon those who have never doubted the wisdom and lawfulness of eating animal flesh, because they have never been led to consider that any principle could be involved in the matter. A very large number of reasons might be urged, in support of the statement that the practice of eating the flesh of dead animals is morally wrong. The first two, if admitted to be valid, are alone sufficient to justify one in logically holding such a conviction, as to commend themselves to your judgment, as being based upon sound reason and common sense. They are as follows, viz:

First. That as man is stated by the leading scientists of the world to be a frugivorous (or fruit eating) animal, not possessing either teeth suitable for tearing flesh, or digestive organs by nature adapted to its assimilation (both of which are found in all the carnivora). the voluntary consumption of the dead bodies of animals in a civilized country is a violation of one of the fundamental laws governing his being, and, therefore, totally unnecessary.

Second. That the custom of eating flesh involves the infliction of an incalculable amount of suffering and torture upon countless thousands of sentient creatures, such enormities as are daily taking place being utterly unjustifiable, except upon the ground of absolute and unavoidable necessity. As this necessity does not exist, the perpetration of those cruelties is morally wrong, being an outrage upon all humane sentiment, and a violation of the Christian duty of showing mercy to the weak and defenceless. Those who purchase the flesh create the demand, and are aiders and abettors of the evil that is done to gratify their degenerate appetites—being accessories both before and after the fact. That the consumption of animal flesh is the direct cause of an immense amount of human suffering and disease, which afflicts not only the consumer, but their children to the third and fourth generation. That the barbarous practice is detrimental to man. It is to a large extent the cause of crime, and vice, with which our own and other lands are cursed, and no reform at present before the public world produces such permanent benefit to the community as the return to the natural food which was originally designed for man. You will doubtless require evidence in support of these statements, and it shall be placed before you.

In support then of my first statement, which is the most important of all, seeing that if it is established to your satisfaction, it ought not to be difficult to convince you, as earnest men and women, that the wholesale slaughter and abominable cruelties involved in flesh eating are utterly unjustifiable. Let me call first as witnesses some of our leading scientits and medical men.

Proper Diet is the Foundation of Health, Strength, and Long Life. Proper Food gives to the digestive organs the force necessary to assimilate the foods; they give the system the power to expel the waste.

Those whose occupations have little opportunity for outdoor exercise must rely chiefly on proper foods to expel waste and foreign elements. I rely upon fine pure olive oil and the proper food for my good health. Even in diseases like cancer, tumors, ulcers, which are treated on a non-flesh diet, I prescribe, alternate weeks, a change of food. There are the strong muscle foods (oats, rye, and whole wheat meal); and those more easily digested, toasted wheat flakes, barley, white flour, corn meal, rice, sago. As a daily diet the strong muscle foods are adapted to the needs of a physical worker.

Great care should be taken to insure a daily evacuation of the bowels. The bowels' action must be secured by a liberal supply of suitable fruits and vegetables in order to insure uninterrupted health. This is a very important point. When we have learned systematically and constantly to eliminate foreign, waste, and unsound elements from the body, we may feel safe in good health. The maintenance of our right weight will be a help to us in this direction, about two pounds to every inch of height. I am 66 inches and weight 132 pounds.

In answer to many inquiries, I will state how I apply my food to my own needs. I eat to satisfaction, being no advocate of over-eating, still less of stopping short of the body's needs, believing both systems injurious to health—the first by burdening the digestive organs with too much food at a time; other by forcing us to live on our reserve force. I live principally on beans, barley, rice, peas, apples, oranges, vegetables, and soup made of fine olive oil, tomatoes, rice, and onions. I vary my diet to suit my needs. Then I can rely on my body as an engineer relies on a well-made machine with plenty of steam and water. Being free from foreign elements, my body responds as quickly to foods taken. By means of diet one can be made bad looking or youthful looking. A youthful appearance is attained by taking fresh fruits, fresh vegetables, tomatoes, and a little starchy food, and plenty of hot lemonade on going to bed. Too much starch, taken in proportion to the other foods, makes the limbs stiff, with wrinkles and other evidence of premature old age.

"Where Are We?" The attitude of churches towards our movement may not be encouraging, but we mean to persevere with the work to which we have put our hands. We have set before ourselves an ideal, and we mean to do our utmost—if by any fair means we may reach it. Our ideal is to make this Earth Paradise once more. We have heard too much, and too long, of Paradise as a future state, wholly distinct from this world in which, alas! are heard unceasingly, cries of helpless pain, and groans of speechless agony. "Be content with such things as ye have," be content with your unhealthy and debasing surroundings; be content with sweater's wages and abject poverty; be content with bad water and adulterated food; be content with poisoned drink and rotten meat; there is a Paradise beyond! So have we preached, so have we exhorted, and we think God has not been mocked! Can that be Gospel; can that be a message of good news which ignores the physical and social ills of this present time, and bid the wretched, helpless sufferers look forward to golden harps and golden crowns, streets of gold and gates of pearl, beyond the grave? There is no room in the world to-day for a religion of this kind, for a religion which is not human from center to circumference. A religion which is not conspicuously and consistently human, is an impossible religion. My professing Christians, realize this and cast your influence into the scales of justice and mercy to "our little brothers and sisters!" And not Christians only, but all those who call themselves "men," or who call themselves "women!" Oh! that our eyes might see a new Jerusalem here and now; in America without shambles and butchers' shops, a people without consumption, cancer, scrofula, and infectious disease; a day when the needless cry of pain is no longer heard in our land! America.

Most Ills that Flesh is Heir to Due to a Wrong Diet and Overeating. What is of more importance than the maintenance of good health—the basis of a sound mind and a sound body? Old Age: Its Cause and Cure. Wrong Diet the Source of Ill Health. Can We Live a Thousand years. The Great Fascinators are Always Middle-Aged. Experiments and Tests for Ascertaining the Properties and Effects of Various Foods. There are No Secrets in Dietetics. Diet is the Foundation of Health, Strength, Beauty, Youthfulness, and Long Life. How I Regained My Health by Proper Food. The reader may be interested to hear my own experience. I had lost my health. Doctors, drugs, and stimulants gave me no relief; and the future looked very dark to me. The idea appealed to my reason. I had taken an active part in farm-life during my youth. I knew that a change of food would affect the milk of the cows. Hence I began to study the subject of correct diet in relation to human beings. Putting the principles I learned into practice, I soon said goodbye to drugs and flesh food; and Dr. Warren too. The doctor then tried to scare me, by saying that in my feeble state of health that I would not live six months on a vegetable diet. And that I must have beef tea and roast beef to build me up. I did not scare worth a cent, and after six months regaining my health, I decided to devote my life to unceasing study and practical experiments, and I have arrived at the results given in my book of my perfect health at the Age of One Hundred and Ten Years the first day of last May, 1906. And I work every day and sell my book, for my living, that I have written after I have past my One Hundred and Fifth year, with the fourth edition I have written at Age One Hundred and Ten. Year of Age, May 1, 1906, in perfect health.

Looking at vegetarianism in the light of comparative anatomy it is self-evident that man was designed to be a Vegetarian. Quadrupeds are divided into classes according to their foods, and with the single exception of man, no animal as a class has ever varied from the design of nature. Those classes are the carnivorous or flesh eating, the fruit eating, the grass eating, and the omnivorous. Each of those classes has distinctive organs adaptable to the digestion of the kind of food it eats, and to no other kinds.

Man has artificially become an omnivorous animal in spite of the fact that anatomically he is a fruit-eating animal. It is an amusing and significant fact that the only typical omnivorous animal is the pig. Man is trying hard to be a pig.

The carnivorous animals all have very short intestines, adapted only to the digestion of meat. They have only one stomach and could not digest grass as the cow does. Their teeth are all long and sharp, so that they can tear meat, but they have no flat-topped teeth to grind vegetable foods as man has. It has been said that the so-called "canine" teeth of man are like those of the carnivorous animal. This is not correct, strictly speaking. To be sure, they are somewhat pointed, but they are also flat at the point. They are not round and pointed, like those of the carnivorous animals. The grass-eating animals have several stomachs—from two to five—and very long intestines, especially adapted to the digestion of grass. They have also flat-topped teeth for grinding.

The fruit-eating animals are the only ones that resemble man. They have only one stomach and a medium length alimentary canal, half way between that of the carnivorous and the grass-eating classes. The nearest animal to man is the monkey and the ape. They are fruit-eaters. No meat-eating animal in the world has the horizontal movement of the lower jaw in eating as man has. This is proof positive that man is not a meat-eater, according to the design of nature. These arguments on the physical side of the question prove primarily that man is not physically adapted to the eating of meat. When we eat meat we are eating the product of the earth at second hand. The vegetation has been eaten by the animal, and a large part of it converted into bone and tendon and wasted, and we eat only what is left and made into diseased flesh. That it is especially a stimulant rather than a food, and that there is great danger of the transmission of various serious diseases from animal to man. Scrofula, cancer, ulcer, tumors, boils, eruptions, indigestion, fever, rheumatism, headache and gout. Meat-eating in the ideal stage is bad enough. If the animals that we eat were in all the health which nature endows them roaming wild and free over the open fields, with plenty of exercise, and permitted to choose of their own free will from the best of the various vegetable growths for their food, that would be quite another thing. But as civilization has advanced, cattle are raised for the sole purpose of slaughter, they get little or no exercise.

Any veterinary surgeon will tell you that animals kept without exercise will contract and propagate various diseases which are practically unknown to them in their wild state. They are artificially fattened, and this kind of fat is not the sort of material which we should put into our bodies. It is food for Insane, Murder and Suicide.

OLD AGE: ITS CAUSE AND CURE.

We have been taught to believe that we are in our prime at thirty-five or forty years of age; that we must expect in later years minor or greater ailments. We must be stiff and old, to have gray hair, wrinkles, etc. Women are cautioned to be careful at the "change of life," as otherwise they will incur serious discomforts. Deafness, blindness, loss of memory, and other causes of old age are considered, like the headaches to which all add to necessary evils. But this need not be so if we take rejuvenating foods, as a combination of fine pure olive oil, vegetables, and fruits taken with starchy foods. The retention of waste, foreign, or unsound elements, the undigested portion of our food which the system has been unable to expel, is the principal cause of premature old age and disease. Starch, being hard of digestion, and constipating, if taken in excess, will prevent the elimination of those foreign elements, and for this reason a proper diet should contain only so much starch as would keep the muscularly strong. With fine pure olive oil, I do believe that diet is the chief factor in the production of lasting good health. For the most part of those who now pride themselves on their health, they do not know why they are in health. If they knew how to keep their health, they would surely do so. There would be fewer suffering old men, women and children, if they took proper food; for a beautiful skin, bright eyes, and a fresh body can never be unattractive. It is lost sooner or later, and leaves the possessor disappointed. When, however, we have learned to keep off old age, we shall be able to attract such surroundings, such conditions of existence, as will assure us permanent happiness.

ARE ANIMALS IMMORTAL?

By Josiah Oldfield, M. A., L. R. C. P., M. M. C. S.

The commonest excuse for taking the life of an animal is "that it has no soul." Is this true? And if so, how do we know it? Revealed religion does not say so. It is only dogma of ignorant selfishness which can defiantly, emphatically say, "Animals have no hereafter." Many a nation—aye, one as highly developed as the Jewish in the time of the Maccabees—has denied that women are fit to enter the heavens of the blessed, and if they have a future at all, it must be in the Gehenna of destruction. "Animals have no consciousness of a future life, and therefore have no future life." Does this follow? There are, and have been, races of men who have had no consciousness of a future life; have they, because of that, no future life? Do those who claim the Deity to man because of his consciousness after life, deny it to those who, in a fixed creed of atheism, have no belief in a soul entity apart from a chemical vitality? Would they deny a future existence to idiots and lunatics on the ground of inability, to formulate through which can be projected beyond the limit of temperal existence? I think not. Why then should such arguments be valid in the case of lower animals? Let us take one of the most striking arguments in favor of human existence after death—the incompleteness and consequent injustice of the present life, considered as the totality of human existence.

A child is born into the silence and darkness of a living tomb, sightless, dumb, deaf, and often suffering daily pain. The poor creature mysteriously, comes into this world and lives on in patient, protracted, existence until, as an old man, this mockery of a man passes beyond the veil. Now I ask the skilled Christian teacher what are you going to do for this tortured soul? The first lesson taught is bad "God is Love." This looks to me a gaunt lie, a staring skeleton of hypocrisy, if this life were all.

Too much care cannot be exercised in the selection of our foods. Nature provides ample guides in selection of food, but the influence of custom, heredity and erroneous habits has perverted these natural guides, and have become in most cases vitiated and consequently misleading. In selecting our food science of comparative anatomy establishes the fact that man is naturally a grain, fruit and nut eating animal, therefore, if we desire to conform to nature we must observe this fact in the selection of food. Mastication, even with well pulverized food, is important in order to thoroughly mix the saliva with the food, and thus prepare it for the digestive process in the stomach, which consists of a thorough blending of it with the gastric juice. The risk of getting diseased meat as shown by the recent investigation into the beef supply, of the army of the United States and the fact that the flesh even of healthy animals is productive of those diseases caused by a superfluity of uric acid, rheumatism, Bright's disease, headache and various other diseases, is the disobedience of Nature's laws. It is against nature to eat the foods in any other condition than that in which she provides them. Nature does not err. No one can improve upon nature, yet that's what man attempts to do when he subjects his food to the heat of fire; cooking food is destroying its vitality and changing its value, and the purpose of the product of Mother Earth given to us for sustenance are uncooked save by the heat of the sun—the source of all energy. The sun is productive of life. Cooking destroys the life cells in food—the cells which make and sustain life in man. Graft a dead cutting to a live limb and see whether it will grow or whether it will help the growth of the live branch. All live vegetation is capable either of reproducing its own kind or of furnishing life or vitality to other organized living things. Take away its life and it can do neither. Life can't come from death. The food that the system cannot expel, this waste material, foments and decays in the stomach or intestines, furnishing food for the germs and baccilli which daily enter the system.

I will simply state that I have, during the past year, taken a very liberal quantity of salt every day, with food at meal times; have also added it to the morning and evening baths, in about the same proportions as it exists in sea water. No unpleasant sensations whatever have been caused as a result, but, on the other hand, physical and nerve force has been increased to a most appreciable extent. I have come across several persons lately, with nervous prostration, and who upon inquiry I found had been abstaining from common salt for a long time. In several cases they fully understood the necessity for what is known as "conservative cookery," and yet they appeared to have suffered from saline starvation.

I have received several letters on the subject of common salt in response to the article I refer to. I haven't any scientific facts in support of the opinion, to prove that chloride of sodium does enter into chemical combination with the potash salts which are absorbed so largely from certain vegetable foods, and are injurious when found in excess in the blood serum. I trust that some of our friends who deprecate the use of common salt will be prepared to come forward with reliable scientific data in support of their position. Should any feel disposed to do so, it would give me pleasure to publish an article on the subject in my next book.

Meanwhile, I will simply state that I have, during the past three months, taken a very liberal quantity of salt every day, both in the form of a solution in the morning and with food at meal times; have also added it to the morning and evening bath in about the same proportions as it exists in sea water. No unpleasant sensations whatever have been caused as a result, but, on the other hand, physical and nerve force has been augmented to a most appreciable extent. I feel the subject is a very important one because I have come across several persons lately, who manifested anaesthetic symptoms, lack of vitality and nervous prostration, and who, upon inquiry, I found had been abstaining from common salt for a long time. In several cases they fully understood the necessity for what is known as "conservative cookery," and yet they appeared to have suffered from saline starvation. The quest after truth in such a matter ought to be placed before any personal considerations, and I trust that some of our medical friends in the Food Reform World will be able to throw light upon this problem. Any experimental information will be welcomed for my next book. All who are in sympathy with the Food Reform, to their friends as being worthy of investigation, I should also feel obliged if they would mention my book, and state where they can be obtained, so that those who feel disposed to look into the matter may have an opportunity of doing so. The Secret of Long Life, by the author of the book (age 110 years) by sending 50 cents, postoffice order, to G. E. D. Diamond, San Francisco, California, and I will send you my book, "Secret of Long Life," to your postoffice address, post paid.

Where are we? Of course, he has been most indignant that his profession should have been criticized, or that anyone should have ventured to expose the evils attendant upon eating dead bodies, and to try and show people that pure air, pure water and pure food form the great elixir of life. When one looks up the subject of allopathic medicine, one is astonished to find what little ground even Medico has to stand upon, for we find Sir Astley Cooper saying, "The science of medicine is founded on conjecture and improved by murder," and Professor Gregory, of the Edinburgh Medical College, saying: "Gentlemen, ninety-nine out of every hundred medical facts are medical lies, and medical doctrines are, for the most part, stark, staring nonsense;" or, again, Professor F. B. Parker, of New York, states "Instead of investigating for themselves, medical men copy the errors of their predecessors, and have thus retarded the progress of medical science and perpetuated error." Or, in conclusion, Sir John Forbes says "No classification of disease or therapeutic agents ever yet promulgated is true, or anything like truth, and none can be adopted as a safe guide in practice." Then how in the name of common sense should any man do other than welcome new ideas which may help to put his profession on a sounder and more perfect basis? Flesh-eating is unnecessary—man was created a frugivorous animal and not a carnivorous one, and any violation of this primary law of our being will bring with it physical diseases and suffering which all the doctors in the world cannot prevent. A well-known M. D. (Lond) told me a little while ago that it was practically impossible for anyone living on a humane diet to suffer either from rheumatism or Bright's disease. Although close on sixty years of age, he was honest enough to confess that until eighteen months ago he had never given the question of food values any serious attention, and his parting words to me were, "If only people knew what your food reformers are finding out, in a few years' time there would be little need for doctors."

CPSIA information can be obtained
at www.ICGtesting.com
Printed in the USA
BVOW06s0040310717
490676BV00011B/82/P